Uprouse ye then, my barrow-digging men,
It is our opening day!
And all exclaimed, their grog whilst swigging,
There's naught on earth like barrow digging!
Barrow-Digging by a Barrow Knight (1845)

To the memory of my Mother

THE EARLY BARROW DIGGERS

Barry M. Marsden

TEMPUS

First published 1999

PUBLISHED IN THE UNITED KINGDOM BY:

Tempus Publishing Ltd
The Mill, Brimscombe Port
Stroud, Gloucestershire GL5 2QG

PUBLISHED IN THE UNITED STATES OF AMERICA BY:

Tempus Publishing Inc.
2A Cumberland Street
Charleston, SC 29401

Tempus books are available in France, Germany and Belgium
from the following addresses:

Tempus Publishing Group
21 Avenue de la République
37300 Joué-lès-Tours
FRANCE

Tempus Publishing Group
Gustav-Adolf-Straße 3
99084 Erfurt
GERMANY

Tempus Publishing Group
Place de L'Alma 4/5
1200 Brussels
BELGIUM

British Library Cataloguing in Publication Data.
A catalogue record for this book is available from the British Library.

ISBN 0 7524 1427 5

Typesetting and origination by Tempus Publishing.
PRINTED AND BOUND IN GREAT BRITAIN.

Contents

Preface

This book represents an attempt to impart some knowledge regarding the character and work of the eighteenth- and nineteenth-century barrow diggers who, during the 200 or so years covered by this work, were responsible for opening many thousands of ancient burial-mounds distributed throughout England and the rest of Britain. A vastly dissimilar group of individuals, they represented a cross-section of the society of their period.

I hope that this study of early English barrow investigators will cast some light on the activities of this remarkable assembly of clerics, merchants, soldiers, landowners and the like on whose work we have to base so much of our knowledge of Neolithic and Bronze Age society. It does not aim to be a comprehensive history of all the early investigators of tumuli; rather it tries to illuminate certain facets of the lives and endeavours of some of the most important of those researchers into the history of the distant past by the plundering of burial-mounds.

I have tried not to be too harsh on the early investigators. It would be profitless to castigate them for failing to draw accurate contour plans of their barrows, or for not recording by three-dimensional methods. As pioneers they worked according to their own imperfect lights; their techniques gradually improved (though painfully slowly), but only the latest of their breed worked to scientific standards, and recorded their barrows in plan and section. Many of the barrow openers were great collectors, possessing strong acquisitive instincts which led them to amass great assemblages of relics. Many hundreds of them worked in a careless fashion, leaving no account of their labours, and thus denying us the information resulting from the pillaging of innumerable mounds. Many did too much too quickly, again faults of the era in which they lived. But the best of them played their part in helping us to piece together the records of the prehistoric and later past.

The age of the great barrow diggers passed at the end of the nineteenth century. It seems certain that it can never return. Never again will rich, leisured individuals have the time, finances or subjects on which to practise their large-scale depredations. However, those past antiquarians who had the leisure and capital to dig remain very important figures among the piecers-together of our barrow-lore, and as such they deserve some attention and remembrance. I hope this work, its omissions notwithstanding, will help to achieve this aim.

BARRY M. MARSDEN
Eldwick,
West Yorkshire
November 1998.

1 The beginnings of barrow study

Among the wealth of ancient field monuments scattered across the shires of England, the most common and the best-known are barrows, long or circular grass-grown heaps of earth or stones, marking the burial places of prehistoric aristocracy. Some in fact are later in date, as the desire to construct visible monuments over the dead extended into Roman and early Anglo-Saxon times. In places these mounds abound; in other areas they are spread thinly. The best remaining ones to be seen in quantity stand in the great barrow cemeteries of Wessex, though in the past the Yorkshire and Lincolnshire Wolds must have supported large numbers. They still abound in the Peak District, the Cotswolds, Devon, Cornwall and elsewhere, though here more usually in smaller numbers. In other stretches of the country barrows are completely absent, sometimes due to destruction during the past few centuries, or because the locations in question were not amenable to early settlement.

For many centuries after they had been so laboriously piled up, these minor monuments remained in peace, an integral part of the landscape in which they stood. The only stirrings of interest regarding their contents in early days occurred in Roman times when certain mounds in Derbyshire, Somerset and the Mendips were cut into, most probably in a search for curios. The earliest barrow diggings, inspired, it seems, by motives other than treasure-seeking, appear to date from Norman times, when a now vanished barrow group, the 'Hills of the Banners', near Redbourn, Hertfordshire, was attacked by the monks of St Albans. They disinterred and sanctified some nameless Anglo-Saxon whom they took for St Amphibalus, converter of St Alban, the first British Christian martyr. The bones were piously removed to the Abbey church and a shrine was built to receive them. In 1199 a barrow at Ludlow, perhaps a chambered one, since the contemporary account mentions *tria mausolea lapidia* was partly removed to faciliate the extension of the church. Three skeletons were uncovered, and immediately hailed by the clergy as three Irish saints. Their bones were buried in the church 'with the confidence that their holiness would be soon evinced in numerous miracles'.

The exalted motives of these early excavators were paralleled by other barrow diggings undertaken not for spiritual but for pecuniary objectives. Thus a number of barrows in medieval times were ransacked in the search for treasures. These searches were often ordered or blessed by royalty. In 1237 Henry III authorised his brother, the Earl of Cornwall, to dig into Cornish barrows, on terms apparently previously applicable to some diggings in the Isle of Wight. In 1324 Robert Beaupel received permission to dig specific barrows in Devon, probably the Chapman barrows near Challacombe, for treasure. Lord Curzon gained an authorisation to dig for wealth, almost certainly in barrows in 1521 in the counties of Norfolk and Suffolk, and William Digges of Barham in east Kent opened, on Henry VIII's instructions, a large mound on his estate, close to Watling Street. He dug out a large urn 'full of ashes and bones of the largest size, with brass and iron helmets and shields of an unusual bigness'. In the later years of the sixteenth century the Sutton Hoo ship-barrow was cut into, perhaps by Dr John Dee. Fortunately for posterity the diggers lost heart when their central shaft had all but penetrated to the relic chamber.

In 1621 'certain commissioners with the broad seal of England' came to dig at Upwey in Dorset for 'some treasure that lies underground'. After three days of fruitless work, during which 'nothing but a few bones' turned up, they left to dig at Bincombe. Later in the century Sir Thomas Browne's sonorous prose records the finding of 40 or 50 'sad and sepulchral pitchers', burial urns of Saxon date found in a flat cremation cemetery in a field near his home at Old Walsingham, in Norfolk. In common with the practice of the time he regarded the urns as Roman.

Apart from these few examples of medieval and early modern barrow-digging, barrows were recognised and noted by certain writers. From Tudor times Englishmen, influenced by the stimulus of the Renaissance, began to pay heed to the history of their own nation and mentioned the presence of ancient earthworks, including numerous barrows seen by them in various parts of the country. Thus John Leland, after excursions on Salisbury Plain, records the 'sepultures of men of warre ... in divers places of the playne'. Camden notes that 'artificial hills both round and pointed are to be seen in these parts, and are called burrowes or barrowes ... bones are found in them.' Leland also noted in Doddington, Gloucestershire, 'pottes exceding finely nelyd and florished in the Romanes tymes digged out of the groundes in the feldes'.

Early writers suggested a military origin for the barrows they observed, concluding that they covered the remains of individuals slain in Romano-British or Saxo-Danish conflicts. John Aubrey, in his *Monumenta Britannica* refers to them as 'the mausolea or burying-places for the great persons and rulers of the time', although elsewhere in his work he evidently regarded them as marking the sites of battles:

> (Where) so many heroes lie buried in oblivion, and show the greatness of the slaughter. By them may be presumed whereabout the engagement began and which way the victor pursued . . .

He included some pertinent observations on the round barrows he saw. 'Some around Stonehenge', he wrote, 'have circular trenches about them, and the trench is distant from the barrow.' He noted the form of disc barrows, but was undecided about the significance of the central tump, as to whether it covered a burial or served as a platform for 'the priest or general to make an harangue'.

At the beginning of the sixteenth century, Sir John Oglander of Nunwell in the Isle of Wight wrote:

> you may see divors buries on ye topp of oure Island hills . . . being places onlie weare men were buryed. . . I have digged for my experience in soome of ye moore awntientest, and have found manie bones of men formerlye consumed by fyor, according to ye Romane custome.

1 *William Camden (1561–1623), schoolmaster, whose* Britannia *of 1586 was the first archaeological best-seller, and the earliest popular work to mention barrows and barrow groups.*

2 *William Stukeley (1687–1765), doctor, cleric and first of the great English field archaeologists. He was one of the pioneers of barrow digging for the purpose of gaining knowledge of past societies. (Friends of the Ashmolean Museum)*

By the beginning of the eighteenth century barrows were recognised as the burial places of the ancient inhabitants of Britain. However, as few had been dug into for the purposes of gleaning information on their origins and affinities by examination of their remains and gravegoods, the derivation and period of the monuments remained vague and shadowy, and their age a guess. Some light was thrown on the subject by William Stukeley (1687–1765), who between 1719 and 1743 conducted fieldwork in Britain which led to his amassing a collection of notes and sketches dealing with a large number of prehistoric antiquities. Stukeley is regarded as the first great English field archaeologist and antiquarian pioneer. His acute observation and recording contributed much to the growing interest in archaeological field studies, although in later life a wayward imagination peopled his world with Druids, bards and priests, leading to the Druid cult which bedevilled English archaeology for the next century and more. He even turned his field notes into religious tracts to support his weird fantasies. Stukeley sketched many barrows and barrow groups, attempting some classification of them by form, insisting, however, on a variety of peculiar labels including 'kings' barrows', 'archdruids' barrows', and 'priestesses' barrows'. He thought a series of bronze axes, which he described, were used by Druids to hook mistletoe from sacred groves! The wild imaginings besetting him in later life have clouded the value of his early work, and later antiquaries have regarded him as 'a mixture of minute original observation with crude and ill-founded conjecture and hypothesis'.

Stukeley's keen perception enabled him to make sound observations on the barrows around Stonehenge and elsewhere, including the realisation that many enjoyed a 'false crest' siting. He noted that:

> the barrows on Hakpen Hill and others are set with great art not on the very highest part of the hills but upon so much of the declivity or edge as that they make app(earance) as above to those in the valley.

On Oakley Down, Dorset, he showed the 'Ackling Dyke' Roman road to postdate the barrow group there, as it cut through two disc barrows. He wrote:

> The line or direction of the Roman road necessarily carried it over part of one of these tumuli, and some of the materials of the road are dug out of it; this has two little tumps in the centre.

Stukeley set out to 'oblige the curious in the Antiquitys of Britain' and in the 1720s, with financial assistance and prompting from Lord Pembroke, carried out perhaps the first objective barrow diggings on record. He carefully noted the structure of a twin bell barrow in the Cursus group, north of Stonehenge. He wrote:

> The manner of composition of this barrow was good earth, quite thro', covering it quite over under the turf. Hence it appears that the method of making these barrows was to dig up the turf for a great space round till the barrow was brought to its intended bulk. Then with the chalk, dug out of the environing ditch, they powdered it all over . . . About three feet below the surface was a layer of flints, humouring the convexity of the barrow . . . This being about one foot thick, rested on a layer of soft mould another foot; in which was inclos'd an urn full of bones.

Stukeley's conclusions followed:

> It was reasonable to believe, that this was the sepulture of a man and his wife; and that the lesser [barrow] was the female: and so it prov'd, at least a daughter ... It appears to have been a girl of about fourteen years old, by their bulk and great quantity of female ornaments mix'd with the bones, all of which we gather'd. Beads of all sorts ... many in long pieces notch'd between so as to resemble a string of beads, and these were generally of a blue colour (evidently faience). There were many of amber, of all shapes and sizes ... one of these was cover'd with a thin film of pure gold.

In the companion western mound, an intrusive skeleton was disinterred. Stukeley felt this to be the father of the female in the eastern barrow! The primary interment in this barrow was never reached; it was discovered about 80 years later by William Cunnington. Stukeley appended a drawing of a section of the eastern barrow, possibly the first ever recorded by an English prehistorian.

In his writings Stukeley makes mention of further barrow excavations he pursued around Stonehenge and Avebury. 'In a great and old fashioned barrow, west from Stonehenge', he wrote, 'I found bits of red and blue marble chippings of the stones of the temple, so that, probably, the interred was one of the builders', proving the contemporaneity of the barrow and the 'bluestone' phase of the henge, or a period when the bluestones were being re-used. He also dug into some 'Druid' (disc) barrows at Normanton, including one 'next to bush barrow, westward of it'. He found a chalk-cut grave with a cremation. Of disc barrows he noted that 'there is commonly an urn' under the 'small tump of earth in the middle'. At Windmill Hill, he opened a small barrow, 'very old, flat and round, and found an entire urn turned upside-down, into a hole cut in the solid chalk. The bones very rotten'. From other notes mentioning further barrows he opened, one gains the impression that Stukeley was for a time very active among the Wiltshire barrows on Salisbury Plain. In fact, he hired labourers to dig for him at certain times. He mentions one, 'Richard Hayns, an old man of Ambresbury, whom I employed to dig for me in the barrows'. Stukeley heard that Hayns had reputedly found Roman coins in the Stonehenge barrows, and was selling them at inflated prices. He himself doubted that the coins had come from the reputed source, feeling Hayns to be guilty of sharp practice; as he wrote, 'I suspect he pretended to find them at Stonehenge, only for the sake of the reward'!

Although Stukeley took care to note 'how the body was posited' in his examination of skeletons, he often failed to reveal where it was 'posited', thus failing to appreciate the significance of primary, secondary and intrusive interments. Nevertheless as the first purposeful digger for knowledge Stukeley is an important figure; he serves to mark the transition between untested theory and questing investigation.

2 Early explorers

In the middle and later years of the eighteenth century two enthusiasts emerged to dispel some of the darkness surrounding the nature of certain of the barrows in south-east England. They were the Reverend Bryan Faussett and the Reverend James Douglas. Their researches were pursued almost entirely among the then vast Anglo-Saxon barrow cemeteries scattered in clusters across the Downs. Both men were, in certain respects, in advance of their time. Douglas's great work, *Nenia Britannica*, first printed as a series of supplements, was poorly received despite its great merit, and Faussett's manuscript *Inventorum Sepulchrale* did not become available as a printed work until 1856. Indeed Faussett's vast collection of Saxon antiquities was but little known until its exhibition at the Canterbury Congress in 1844. It was then offered, for a moderate sum, to the Trustees of the British Museum, who, to their eternal shame, refused it!

Bryan Faussett (1720–76), born at Heppington, Canterbury, was the eldest of 13 children. In 1730, at the age of 10, he watched with avid interest the digging of a group of Saxon barrows on Chartham Downs in east Kent by Cromwell Mortimer, a well-known antiquary and one of those responsible for the refounding of the Society of Antiquaries in 1717, though he was also described as an 'impertinent, assuming, empyric physician'. Mortimer regarded the barrows as covering those slain in a battle between Julius Caesar and the Britons. He recorded his excavation in a turgid and laborious narrative, but his description of the relics was, for its time, excellent.

Faussett attended University College, Oxford, where he gained some notoriety as a Jacobite supporter (his father convened secret meetings of Jacobite gentry in his home village) during the risings of 1745–6. Faussett gained his MA in 1745 and was ordained in 1746. In later years he was to regret having taken holy orders. From 1757 to his death he devoted his attentions to the study of Kentish antiquities, particularly barrows. His first barrow diggings were at Tremworth Downs, Crundale, where his careless workmen smashed many pottery vessels. For his period, Faussett was a careful, painstaking observer whose main aim was to satisfy a thirst for knowledge. He kept a daily illustrated journal of his work. One of his hopes was to prove that the burials in the Kentish grave-clusters 'were not slain in battle, as many have erroneously surmised, but that they were ... neither more nor less than the peaceable inhabitants of the neighbouring village or villages'.

Thus this churchman-antiquary became an informative pioneer of early archaeology, although he failed to recognise the period of his discoveries, referring to the skeletons he found as 'Britons Romanised' or 'Romans Britonised'. His journal, edited and published in 1856, was a valuable and entertaining work. One amusing incident, Faussett recalls, occurred at Gilton near Sandwich. He travelled there in 1759, examining and recording church memorials and enquiring about local antiquities. He was directed to a sandpit

3 *Bryan Faussett (1720–76), Kentish antiquary and collector, who during his lifetime dug into nearly 800 Anglo-Saxon barrows in his native county. (Merseyside Museums)*

where apparently during digging, or after frost or rain had caused subsidence, 'many antiquities of different sorts' had been picked up by farm-workers or the servants of the miller who owned two windmills on the west side of the pit. Faussett records:

> I immediately visited the place, and after having looked about it and examined it for some little time, one of the miller's servants came into the pit to me and shewed me something sticking out, about three or four inches out of the sand, about three feet from the surface of the eastern and deepest part of the pit. It appeared to me to be nothing more than some piece of stick or some root: but he assured me it was the head of a spear: and said he was certain there was a grave there from the colour of the sand, which in a small line of about eighteen inches in length, and parallel to the surface and about two inches in thickness, appeared in that place of a much darker tinge than the rest of the sand. He told me also, that, if I were pleased he would get a ladder and a spade and see what was in it.
>
> It was pretty late in the day, which made me object to his proposal, imagining

> that he would not have time to go through with his work. However, on his assuring me that he had been used to the work, and that by the help of another miller, his fellow-servant, he should soon rifle it (for that was his expression), my curiosity prompted me, though at a considerable distance from home, to set them about the business and to wait the event.
>
> The miller and his companion immediately produced two ladders and as many spades; and with these began to delve in a very rough manner into the sand rock in a horizontal manner, as if they had designed to have made an oven. The head of the spear (for such indeed it proved) they, at the first or second stroke of their spades, contrived to break all to pieces. Indeed it was very brittle. At the next stroke or two, part of a skull and a few vertebrae of the neck (all much decayed) were indiscriminately with the soil cast down into the pit, without the least care or search after anything. That concern, they said, they left to me and my servant at the bottom, who were nearly blinded with the sand falling on us, and in no small danger of being knocked on the head, if not absolutely buried, by the too zealous impetuosity of my honest labourers.
>
> I found, in short, that this method of proceeding would not do; but that if the grave did chance to contain anything curious, it must, most likely, be lost and overlooked. I therefore desired them to desist, and advised them rather to open the ground above, till they should get down to the skeleton, and then carefully to examine the bottom of the grave. This advice, having been used to proceed oven-fashion, if I may so call it, they did not at first at all relish: but after a little persuasion and a little brandy (without which nothing, in cases such as the present, can be done effectually), they very cheerfully approved and very contentedly followed, so that in a very short time they got to the skeleton, I mean to what remained of it. And though I then went into the grave myself, and very carefully examined every handful of the above mentioned discoloured sand (namely, where the body had lain and rotted), I found nothing but some soft spongy remains of decayed bones. It was now too near night to think of doing anything more at that time, and too late in the season, to attempt anything further that year. But I promised myself the pleasure of returning to the work, and making a further and more diligent search, as early as the weather and length of days of the ensuing spring would give me leave.

Faussett's main fault as an archaeologist was of course the fault of his and subsequent ages, that of attempting far too much in far too short a time. Hence at Gilton he opened 106 barrows in 11 days spread over the years 1760, 1762 and 1763. At Kingston Down he dug 308 barrows between August 1767 and 1773. Between 1771 and 1773 he also dug 366 barrows in various other localities in Kent. His final total was some 777 barrows. His one-day record of openings appears to be 31, on 29 July 1771. A few days previously, on 16 July, he dug nine barrows in two hours, at Bishopsbourne near Canterbury! The mounds were situated close by the main road and Faussett determined on an early start, otherwise by their proximity to a public way 'I know myself liable to be pestered with a numerous set of troublesome spectators' — a *cri de coeur* to be oft repeated in these pages. He wrote,

> So setting ourselves immediately to the business we finished our work in little more than two hours; during which time we had very little or no interruption, either from the curiosity or impertinence of passengers, or other idle spectators, the teazingness and plague of whose ill-timed attendance in business of this sort, is not to be conceived but by those who, like myself, have had the disagreeable experience of it.

Faussett was not a rich man, and he often made monetary sacrifices in order to dig. His supervision of barrow openings was carried out with 'almost boyish enthusiasm' and, like many barrow diggers to follow, he clearly derived great pleasure from his work. One of his most important finds was the Kingston disc-brooch, 3in in diameter and ornamented with gold, garnets and turquoises. It was actually picked up by his son Henry, 'born and bred an antiquary', who excitedly bore it to his father who was resting in his coach, suffering an attack of gout, a disease he became martyr to in the last 20 years of his life. Faussett drove off with the brooch and next day the local villagers spread a report that he had departed with such a load of gold that the coach-wheels would hardly turn. Whereupon the lord of the manor prohibited all further excavations on his property!

After Faussett's death, his superb collection, containing 400 jewels alone, remained in obscurity at Heppington until the 1844 Canterbury Congress of the British Archaeological Association revived interest in it. In 1853 the British Museum incredibly refused to purchase it when it was offered for sale and it eventually went to Joseph Mayer's Museum in Liverpool. The latter ensured that Faussett's manuscript was edited and published by Roach Smith, some 80 years after the antiquary's death. The assemblage can now be seen in Merseyside Museum.

The torch lit by Faussett was kept alight after his death by the Reverend James Douglas (1753–1819). Born in London, he was the youngest of nine children, and under the influence of an elder brother he was placed in business with a successful manufacturer in Middleton, Lancashire. However, Douglas found the attractions of the nearby museum of Sir Ashton Lever (a wealthy industrialist with a taste for collecting) much more congenial than business, and he developed a flair for pursuits other than the cotton industry. His family strongly disapproved and he was removed to Leghorn in Italy to act as business agent for his elder brother, to prepare and introduce him to a career in commerce. For one reason or another, and accounts vary, things worked out badly and he was again removed, this time to a military college in Flanders, somewhat in disgrace. He took to the life, eventually entering the Austrian army. He was stationed in Vienna, and in due course was sent on a mission to England to buy horses. Rumours of a possible Austro-Turkish war caused him to remain in his native land, since, he felt, the thought of his head on the gates of Constantinople 'would not be a very becoming sight'.

Good fortune again attended him, as after a short sojourn in Cambridge (1777) family influence bought him a lieutenancy in the Leicester Militia. Douglas had some considerable skill in draughtsmanship and the art of fortification (he translated de Guilbert's *Essay on Tactics*), and his reputation led to a commission in the newly formed Corps of Engineers who were remodelling the great earthworks across the chalk downs of the Chatham Lines, protecting the Medway estuary and Chatham dockyard. The great

4 *James Douglas (1753–1819), one of the finest antiquarian scholars of his day. His fame rests on his pioneering* Nenia Britannica, *and his contribution to some of the principles of modern archaeological thought. (Friends of the Ashmolean Museum)*

scars cut across the downs frequently revealed relics of the past, and the discovery of these whetted Douglas's taste for antiquities. He commenced 'ransacking' a group of small mounds, with his Colonel's blessing, using sappers and digging during official working hours! The investigations doubtless began as mere treasure hunting and were in all probability hasty and rough, although Douglas kept careful notes, sketches and illustrations of the objects uncovered; he did in fact produce one of the earliest ground plans of an excavated burial mound known to English archaeology. On one occasion, called from his repast by three excited Irish sappers on their report of finding a giant skeleton, he arrived at the barrow, breathless and full of expectation, to find the Saxon's bones to be of normal size. With a terrifyingly unarchaeological disregard for the remains

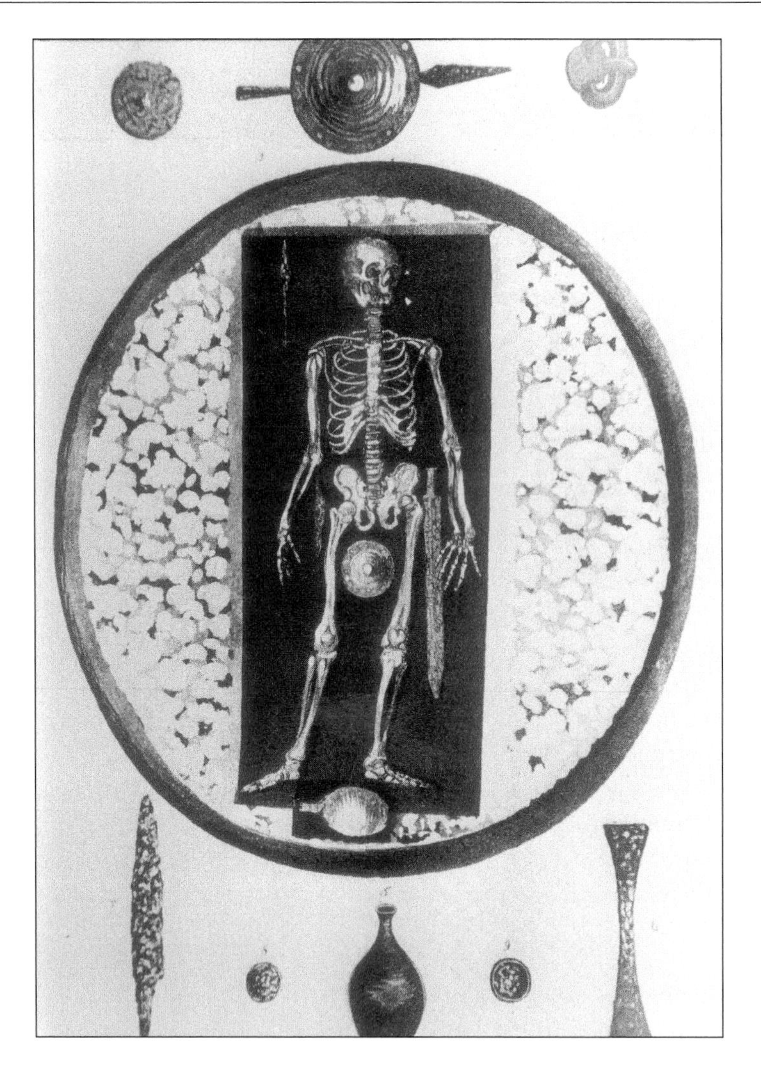

5 *Plan of Tumulus 1 on the Chatham Lines, opened by Douglas in 1779, the first ground plan of a barrow known to British archaeology.*

of the long-defunct warrior. Douglas began 'belabouring' the unfortunate sappers with a thigh bone 'for their natural promptness to magnify these casual discoveries into the marvellous'!

With the free labour so generously provided by the army, Douglas soon amassed a considerable collection and his fame began to spread. By 1780 he was married and living in Rochester. By the end of the Anglo-French war he had determined to leave the army and pursue the study of antiquities which had become almost his main *raison d'être*. He next decided, quite casually it would seem, to enter the church, although in his subsequent career he failed conspicuously to gain preferment as a priest, though he strove incessantly to achieve this. The main reason for his failure appears to stem from a paper he read to the Royal Society. In it he advanced the 'heresy' that the bones of a mammoth found 12ft deep in undisturbed sand and gravel by the Medway at Chatham were of vast age and precluded the idea of a universal deluge in the Medway valley. Since the general body of the established church accepted Archbishop Ussher's date of 4004 BC for the creation of the world, Douglas's ideas represented an unacceptable deviation from established beliefs and henceforth, church preferment was denied him.

His greatest archaeological work, commenced in the early 1780s, was a general history of the funeral customs of the Ancient Britons, illustrated by numerous plates and intended as a series of supplements, available by subscription. The scope of the work ranged from the 'Celtic' to the 'Danish' periods, and it was entitled *Nenia Britannica*. The first number appeared in May 1786, delayed by a drunken artist who cut off the tops and bottoms of some of the drawings. Issue five was published by late 1787, but subsequent parts were badly delayed to Douglas's 'confusion, loss, disappointment and . . . unspeakable trouble'. He particularly blamed the booksellers whom he felt had 'shamefully spoiled and neglected' his *magnum opus*. The complete work was not available until 1793, but despite its obvious merit, was poorly received simply because it was well ahead of its time. Not until 1835 did a writer extend it the commendation it deserved.

Douglas hoped that his book would repair his fortunes, but this it singularly failed to do. It did however seriously undermine his health, especially his eyes which suffered from the fumes given off by the acid he used in engraving the copper plates for the illustrations. His general constitution also faltered under violent chills and fevers, influenza and severe colds which frequently confined him to bed for long periods. In later years he met both Hoare and Cunnington, accompanying them on barrow-digging excursions on the Wiltshire downs. He also corresponded with other antiquaries such as Henry Godfrey Faussett, and Hayman Rooke, who was busy recording his delvings into the barrows in the Derbyshire Peak.

Continuing disfavour with church authorities forced Douglas into a quiet retirement occupied in writing and dealing in paintings. Latterly he served as chaplain to the 10th Royal Hussars, the Prince of Wales's own regiment, at Brighton. He occasionally dug on the Sussex downs using troops from Preston barracks, Chatham, where he died. On his death his valuable collection passed to Sir Richard Colt Hoare who presented it to the Ashmolean Museum, Oxford, where it now reposes. His epitaph in St Peter's Church, Preston, notes that his pioneering volume 'has most learnedly explained all that relates to the burial of the early inhabitants of Britain'. It concludes fittingly, 'He was a disturber, though not without reverence, of other men's sepulchres. May he, in his own, rest quietly'.

Although the work of Faussett and Douglas was pursued only among pagan Saxon barrows, it represented the first full-time, systematic effort to glean some knowledge of the past by the opening of many hundreds of burial mounds. With its many imperfections, it was important both for its own sake — many of the barrows they dug have long since been destroyed and their contents would have been lost — and for stimulating later antiquaries into an interest in the field monuments of their own land.

3 Figures in a Wiltshire landscape

Apart from the investigations of Faussett and Douglas in south-east England, the field of English barrow-study remained fallow for half a century after Stukeley. Interest in barrows and their contents, gradually stirring in the early nineteenth century, probably arose as an offshoot of the Romantic Movement; this, with its expressions of individuality and intense emotion tended to encourage an already existing morbid interest in mortality and the grave. The intellectual climate of England became enveloped in the 'Gothick' cult. Barrows on blasted heaths became objects for aesthetic satisfaction and speculation. Books on the subject were decorated with withered oaks, dripping grottoes with stark representations of dolmens and stone circles in the background. The bones of the prehistoric dead became as one with the features of the rugged landscape so beloved of the Romantic mind. A good example of the cult is shown in the opening pages of Hoare's folios where beads, flints, urns and representations of burial chambers surround the title *Auncient Wiltescire*. Indeed one of the five types of burial mound classified by Hoare was still labelled the 'Druid' barrow. Classical learning and archaeology now had a rival study, and one that could be pursued wholly at home.

It has been suggested more than once that the nineteenth-century barrow diggers evinced a morbid delight in skeletons, graves and mortality that amounted to a gloating over the paraphernalia of death. This is now recognised as a psychological phenomenon that was exploited in the literature and art of the times. Was this why barrows suffered so much from wholesale assaults during this period, while living sites remained almost untouched? Perhaps living sites were then as now most difficult to find, while barrows, as the most easily recognised field monuments, were the handiest subjects for attacking and rifling. The early diggers also had strong acquisitive instincts; many of them made few if any notes of their work, their main concern being to adorn display cases and mantelpieces with ancient pots, flints and trinkets. They had little feeling for the historical importance of the sites they so wantonly ransacked.

Barrow digging was elevated to a science, albeit an inexact one, in the earliest years of the nineteenth century, by the work of the 'fathers of the exploration of barrows', Sir Richard Colt Hoare and William Cunnington. Sir Richard, perhaps inveigled into the realms of prehistory by certain aspects of the Romantic Movement, published his researches in the splendidly produced folios of those two fine volumes, *The Ancient History of Wiltshire*. His collaborator, Cunnington, was responsible for supervising most of the barrow digging, while Hoare provided the capital and labour for opening the 465 mounds they disturbed.

Sir Richard (1758–1838) was the son of a wealthy banker; early in life he inherited large estates and riches. Educated privately, he entered the family banking house. He interested himself in classical studies and his writings show a notable literary ability and a keen appreciation and knowledge of classical literature; he was also a competent artist, a patron of the arts, and a considerable connoisseur.

His marriage in 1783 was cut tragically short by the death of his wife and infant son in 1785. To alleviate his grief, he embarked on two grand tours of Europe which lasted six years, until the French Revolution compelled him to return home. On his travels he visited most continental countries and spent much time in serious study and exploration of classical antiquities. He described and sketched many of them, later publishing an account of his journeys. His romantic leanings next led him to tour Wales and Monmouthshire, the stark, rugged landscape providing an outlet for his emotions. In fact he visited the principality on 14 occasions. He later visited Ireland for much the same reasons. Thus when he finally turned himself to the notable antiquities of his own county he was able to combine in his studies a wide literary skill and a considerable ability and experience in field observation and description, admirably complementing Cunnington's own virtues.

William Cunnington (1754–1810) stood on a considerably lower social plane than his patron. Born in Northamptonshire, circumstances forbade him any opportunity to pursue a higher education, though his active mind and studious, inquiring nature, assisted by wide reading, developed his interest in antiquity and geology. Richard Fenton later wrote of him that he 'displayed very considerable powers of mind, as well as originality ... and left us in admiration of acquirements so rarely met with in men of his rank and calling'. He moved to Heytesbury, Wiltshire, as an apprentice in the woollen trade, and in 1785 set up in partnership as a draper and wool merchant. Although keenly interested in the ancient field monuments now within easy reach, he determined to set his business affairs on a thoroughly sound basis before devoting himself to archaeology. Thus many years passed before he set out on his campaigns of active research.

Cunnington was never a fully fit man. A martyr to continuous headaches, he was forced out into the open air for recuperation and relaxation. He wrote that his doctors 'told me I must ride out or die — I preferred the former, and thank God, though poorly, I am yet alive'. Modern medical opinion suggests he suffered from acromegaly, caused by an overactive pituitary gland, and which manifests itself in headaches, depression, lethargy and a progressive enlargement of the hands, feet, and facially the brow ridges, nose, lower jaw and lips, characteristics of later portraits such as that of Woodforde's in 1808. Hoare too was partly incapacitated by infirmities, including gout, rheumatism, migraines and deafness — enough to slow down any man, though he battled courageously with these formidable foes for the rest of his life.

As time passed Cunnington cultivated the friendship of neighbouring antiquaries. John Britton, a notable if rather volatile Wiltshire topographer, encouraged his earliest work on local barrows and earthworks. The Wiltshire MP, Henry Penruddocke Wyndham, another keen antiquarian and very interested in long barrows, probably prompted Cunnington's first investigations, commenced 'in the hopes of meeting something which might supersede conjecture'. Other acquaintances were the Reverend William Coxe of Bemerton, who introduced him to the Reverend Thomas Leman of Bath, a classical scholar of great learning, and also to Hoare. Leman exercised a great influence over

6 *Sir Richard Colt Hoare (1758–1838), wealthy baronet who financed the earliest systematic diggings into the barrows of Wessex, and wrote the first regional archaeology,* Ancient Wiltshire.

Cunnington, which only lessened as the latter gained experience through barrow opening. Leman's comments and observations on barrows were based on preconceptions culled from his wide readings; they lacked Cunnington's practical knowledge.

Cunnington, whom Hoare sometimes referred to as the 'Arch Druid', developed a capacity for thorough exploration (for the period) and an attention to detail, coupled with carefully written notes, that was without parallel for its period. The real landmark in Cunnington's career came in 1803, when Coxe arranged for him to meet Hoare. The pair had met briefly before, and Hoare had helped to defray the costs of Cunnington's earlier diggings. Hoare, a great enthusiast, agreed at this meeting to accept all the costs of Cunnington's future work and eventually the pair collaborated in the production of a history of Wiltshire based on their joint researches. The Hoare–Cunnington partnership, although in the first instance one of employer and employee, soon developed into a firm and enduring friendship, relatively unmarred by any disagreements. It says much for both individuals that in an age of strict etiquette and stiff formal codes of social conduct they should have enjoyed such great respect and feeling for one another.

The large-scale historical work planned by Hoare was split into two parts, with Cunnington entirely in charge of the spadework. He had little difficulty in getting permission to dig, although on one foray in search of a barrow, a tenant 'took us all for poachers'. Hoare, who was responsible for surface fieldwork and general descriptions of field antiquities, planned each season's work like a military campaign. His energy and clear-cut method is shown in his letters to Cunnington. He wrote:

> The country between Heytesbury and Tilshead, and between Tilshead and Everley demands particular attention — from hence you will proceed to Upavon and Pewsey, at both of which I find good accommodation may be had ... there are some curious excavations between Lidbury and Everley which must be dug into — for John (one of the regular diggers) must be your constant attendant with his pick-axe, without which nothing positive can be ascertained.

Hoare organised a wide scheme of field operations each year and was never niggardly regarding expenses, even when a site proved destitute of finds.

Cunnington sent details of his excavations in the form of letters which reached Hoare at regular intervals. Cunnington's daughters transcribed copies of these letters and they were eventually bound into three volumes which were later bequeathed to the library of the Wiltshire Natural History and Archaeological Society. Cunnington kept all the materials found during his diggings in a specially erected building, the Moss House or museum in his garden. Eight years after Cunnington's death, Hoare bought all the barrow relics from his family. The sum paid, £200, seems generous when one remembers that the full cost of each and every excavation fell on him.

In the first volume of his work, published in 1810 and dealing with south Wiltshire, Hoare announced in his preface that he hoped 'to throw some new light on the history of those Britons who formerly resided on our hills'. He determined that the only information his work would provide would be the incontrovertible facts provided by his and Cunnington's own researches. 'We speak from facts, not theory,' proclaims his

7 *William Cunnington (1754–1810), the 'ingenious tradesman' and friend of Hoare, who directed the opening of some 450 barrows on behalf of his patron.*

introduction; 'such is the motto I adopt, and to this text I shall most strictly adhere.' He promised:

> I shall describe to you what we have found; what we have seen; in short, I shall tell you a plain unvarnished tale, and draw from it such conclusions as shall appear not only reasonable, but even uncontradictable.

Unfortunately for his hopes of finding information that would prove conclusively the origins of the barrow builders of the Stonehenge plains, Hoare was forced to confess in a footnote to his introduction that:

> After the result of ten years' experience and constant research, we are obliged to confess our total ignorance as to the authors of these sepulchral memorials: we have evidence of the very high antiquity of our Wiltshire barrows, but none respecting the tribes to whom they appertained, that can rest on a solid foundation.

The best he could do was to state, 'I have no doubt but that the greater part of our Wiltshire barrows ... were the sepulchral monuments of the Celtic and first colonists of Britain.' Elsewhere he remarks of the barrows that he 'scarcely knew how to separate the era of the one from the other'. So, in spite of hard work and devotion the pair failed to break down the apparent contemporaneity of pre-Roman burials. They remained stubbornly 'Ancient British'. Cunnington sometimes attempted some dating of his mounds. Generally he felt round barrows were erected between 500 and 1000 BC. The Upton Lovell 'Gold Barrow', he thought, covered a chief, buried 'near the time of Caesar's invasion'. Hoare and Cunnington commenced their vast programme of work with little to guide them. They were real pioneers, opening a whole new area of antiquarian study, with information no longer gleaned from classical learning but from actual research in the field. Hoare wrote, 'I cannot depend on any researches but those made immediately under our own eyes.' They would be wholly dependent on the evidence uncovered and interpreted by themselves.

By present standards their working techniques were execrable, but they must be judged by the times. With little previous work to guide them, their methods were necessarily primitive. They involved either a central shaft excavation down into a selected barrow, or a trench (called a 'cutting' by Hoare) driven in from one side to the barrow centre, sometimes carried through to the opposite edge. A contemporary of Hoare, the Reverend Edward Duke, who dug into some of the barrows of the Lake group in the early nineteenth century (with Cunnington's assistance), described his own opening techniques, remarking that 'a perpendicular shaft sunk into the apex, of a size proportionate to that of the barrow, rarely fails of bringing to light its contents'. Gangs of labourers usually carried out the preliminary digging for Hoare and Cunnington. The latter's chief assistants were Stephen and John Parker, father and son, who lived in Heytesbury. Hoare called them 'our Heytesbury pioneers (in private he called them other things!) . . . of whom we feel much indebted for many interesting discoveries'. It is worthwhile noting that one of Thomas Bateman's keenest employees, his 'distinguished barrow opener', was also named Parker. Apparently Cunnington needed all his undoubted patience with John who was occasionally moody. Hoare disapproved of John's surliness. 'I will have no sulking fits' he wrote to Cunnington, 'he must be in a sweet temper,' although, to be fair, the Parkers were keen workers, enthusiastic enough to explore the countryside for traces of antiquities, on their own account. One of Hoare's friends praised their 'superior skill and alacrity'.

Many years after he had worked for Hoare one of his diggers explained the barrow-opening methods of the time to the Reverend William Collings Lukis:

> Sir Richard stopped at the great house and instructed his men to dig down from the top until they got nearly to the level of the natural soil, when they were to send or wait for him. On his arrival the search was continued, and the cist, if any, examined in his presence.

Hoare distinguished a number of barrow types, less fancifully than Stukeley; among them were the bowl (with its variations, the cone and broad barrows) and the bell, saucer and pond. He referred to the disc barrow as the 'Druid' type, echoing Stukeley, to Thurnam's annoyance. Writing later in the century Thurnam wrote, 'It is much to be regretted that this ill-founded designation . . . should have been adopted by Sir R.C. Hoare.' Thurnam himself gave this type of barrow the 'disc' appellation. Hoare also classified the pottery turned up in the openings. To him, beakers were 'drinking cups', and miniature cups 'incense cups'. The other main pottery type he came across was the 'sepulchral urn'. Significantly the first two labels remained in vogue to the end of the nineteenth century; the last is still in use.

Not all the Hoare–Cunnington barrow openings were satisfactory. Out of 465 attempted, 86 were unproductive, often after great efforts in labour and expense. Hoare's writings are studded with references such as 'the work was attended with much labour and expense', and 'after infinite labour' and so on, the failures recalled with comments like 'we were again foiled' or 'we missed the interment'. In their work the pair realised the distinction between primary and secondary interments — a distinction Stukeley missed altogether. Hoare noted in certain mounds that 'the position of the skeletons so near the surface evidently proves them to have been a subsequent deposit.' However, despite Douglas's important work in Kent, Hoare totally failed to appreciate that some burials he discovered were Anglo-Saxon, despite the clear correlation between the gravegoods he found, and those illustrated from grave mounds in *Nenia Britannica*. Thus of a Saxon interment on Rodmead Down he remarks, 'I see no reason why the barrow might not have contained the remains of a Belgic warrior.' Elsewhere he refers to Saxons as 'Romanised-Britons' or concludes that their era 'cannot be satisfactorily ascertained'.

One of Hoare's greatest virtues was the production of excellent maps and sketches of barrow groups, drawn by his surveyor and steward Philip Crocker. These maps accurately pinpoint the barrows he opened, and provide an example that, unfortunately, many of those who succeeded him in the field of barrow digging in the nineteenth century totally failed to copy. Experience soon led the pair to come to certain conclusions regarding the

8 *Drawings of barrow types found in Wessex, and illustrated in* Ancient Wiltshire.

9 *Examples of lead plaques deposited by Cunnington in barrows opened by him in the early nineteenth century. (Wiltshire Archaeological Museum)*

barrows they opened. For instance, Hoare related that 'experience has taught us that our labour would be thrown away in attempting any barrows in . . . damp situations,' and that quite often the most prolific numbers of burials and finds occurred in the smaller barrows. The largest often contained the most insignificant deposits. One huge mound in the Lake group covered, to Hoare's disgust, only a simple cremation, 15ft below the surface.

Hoare and Cunnington consistently failed to preserve the bones from the graves they cleared out. Thurnam regretted that 'neither Sir Richard Hoare or Mr Cunnington preserved any of the human remains, and especially the skulls, found by them'. In the introduction to *Ancient Wiltshire* Hoare stated his policy towards human remains:

> In the numerous barrows we have opened, due reverence has always been paid to the mighty dead; their bones and ashes have been carefully collected and deposited in the same tomb.

His claim to 'due reverence' seems at variance with one occasion while digging a barrow in the Cursus group, when his party occupied themselves in 'throwing out the bones' of a skeleton, and observing 'how well they are preserved when deposited deep in the chalk, as they would bear being thrown for a considerable distance without breaking'! Thomas Bateman dismissed Hoare's 'costly folios' as 'in a great measure useless to the scientific student' because Hoare did not preserve inhumed bones, hence failing to produce 'any craniological notices or measurements'.

It seems a pity that the skeletal remains from these excavations were not preserved. They would have represented a very important collection of prehistoric material for modern study, to help determine the physical characteristics of the Neolithic and Early Bronze Age inhabitants of Salisbury Plain and elsewhere. Indeed later on in the century Thurnam redug a number of the Hoare–Cunnington barrows to recover the skulls from

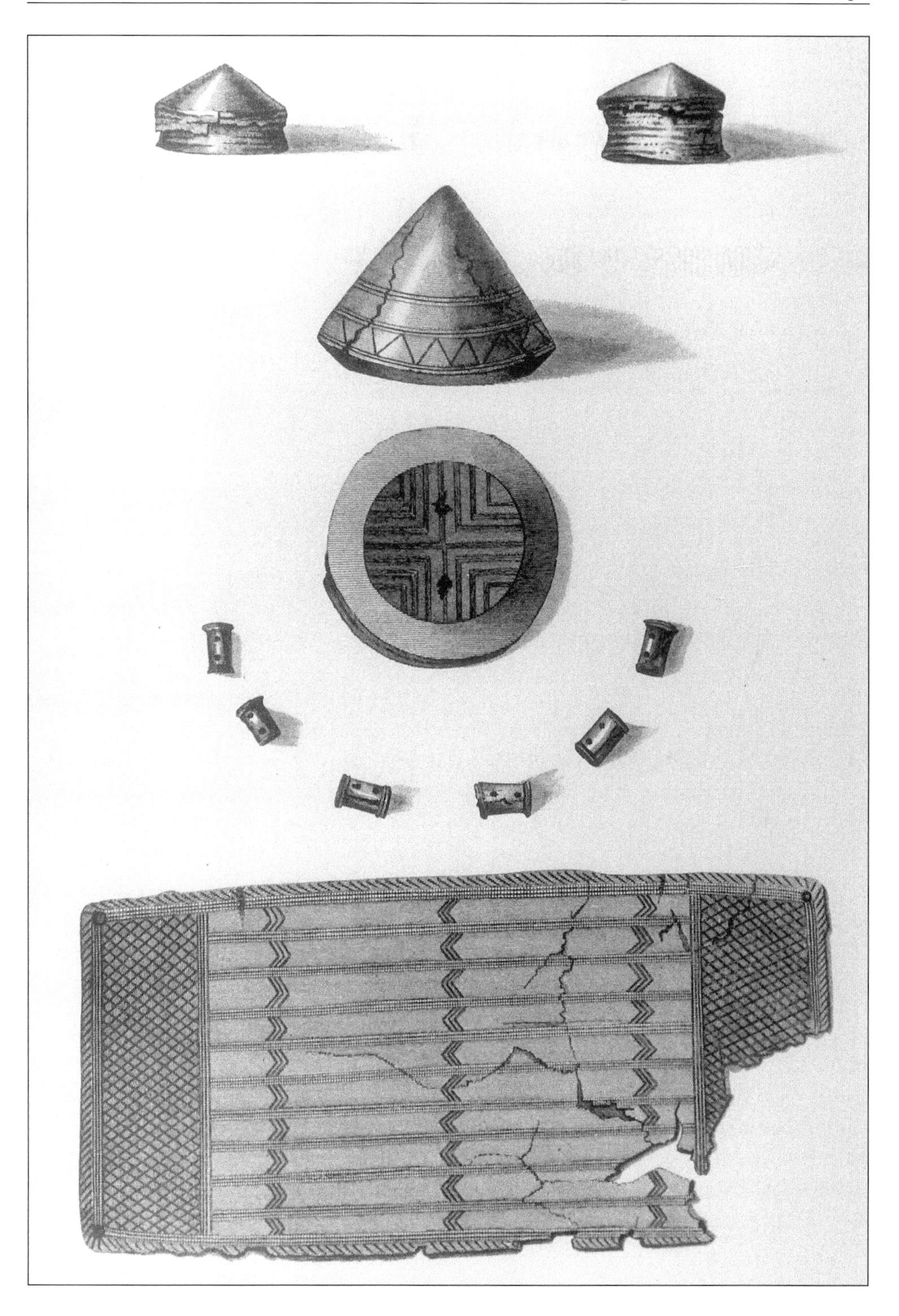

10 *Gold articles from the Upton Lovel 'Gold Barrow', including a thin sheet of incised gold, a gold bound amber button and six cylindrical gold beads.*

them. In an amusing sidelight to his experiences with bones, Hoare recollected uncovering a skeleton in a barrow on Whitesheet Hill. 'Its mouth was open,' he wrote, 'and it grinn'd horribly a ghastly smile, a singularity we have never before met with.' Almost a century later, Pitt-Rivers drily suggested that the skeleton was laughing at Hoare for his unscientific method of dealing with it!

Hoare only added comments about the skeletons he disinterred when he came across something unusual or out of the ordinary. In digging a barrow at Amesbury he wrote that one skull had been trepanned — 'the most remarkable circumstance was finding a piece of the skull, about five inches broad, that had been apparently sawn off.' This roundel of the bone was recovered during a re-excavation of the barrow (Amesbury G51) in 1960. Similarly, he noted an unusual skull type in a long barrow on Normanton Down. 'One of the persons here interred,' he wrote, 'seemed to have no forehead, the sockets of his eyes appearing to have been on top of his head, and the final terminations of the vertebrae turned up.'

Occasionally the pair neglected to recover pottery as well as human remains from their excavations. Crushed beakers and urns, or those smashed by the pickaxe, were sometimes left. For instance in their investigations into the Oakley Down barrow group in Dorset, the base of a large urn, bearing a six-rayed wheel ornamentation, was not preserved, neither was 'a fine urn, probably the drinking cup', in a bell barrow in the same group. This beaker lay broken at the feet of 'a British hero'. At other times, according to Thurnam, they neglected the 'simpler flint objects' deposited in their barrows. It seems incredible, writing from this distance in time, that the pair could be so systematic and careful in some ways, and so careless in others. One great failure was to note in most cases the burial attitude of skeletons they found. Hoare records 80 occasions where inhumations occurred as primary burials. Of these, 10 had been disturbed and of the other 70, he only records the position of the body on 15 occasions, though the argument of silence suggests that the other 55 bodies were crouched, since he invariably wrote of extended burials that they were laid 'contrary to the general custom'.

Hoare often mentioned Stukeley — 'our learned Doctor' — in the pages of his folios. He complained that 'practical experience has shown us in how imperfect and unsatisfactory a manner his researches on barrows were conducted', noting that experience had given Cunnington and himself 'repeated proofs that the system of opening barrows was but imperfectly understood in former days'! Opening a twin barrow on Normanton Down, Hoare discovered that Stukeley had preceded them and had left two halfpennies as tokens, one of William III and one of George I dated 1718. Hoare wrote that 'on meeting with these tokens our labourers left off work thinking that the learned Doctor had been beforehand with us'. Incidentally, Hoare and Cunnington usually left tokens of their own in their barrows. These generally consisted of circular or square pieces of metal stamped 'Open'd by RCH' or W. Cunnington (sometimws 'WC') and often accompanied by the date. This practice was later followed by Bateman and others. Sometimes Hoare left coins — for instance at Oakley Down he 'deposited new Bolton halfpennies, and square pieces of lead, stamped "open'd 1804 WC"'.

The most unsatisfactory and disappointing undertakings experienced by Hoare and Cunnington were carried out on the earthern long barrows scattered across the Wiltshire

11 *Bird's eye view of the barrow cemetery at Winterbourne Stoke, engraved by Crocker and extensively investigated by Cunnington. Practically every type of barrow known in Wiltshire is represented in this group.*

Downs, and whose secrets they could not fathom. A great deal of time, money and effort was spent in attacking these colossal monuments, the workmen often labouring on them for a week or more. The usual opening method was to excavate trenches in the broader, higher ends. Often the local long barrows suffered two or three assaults from the spades and picks of the workforce. Sometimes the work was downright dangerous. Cunnington was obliged to cease his operations at Bowls Barrow, Imber, since the great height of the barrow and the loose nature of its construction caused large stones continually to roll down on the workmen in the trench, threatening life and limb.

The pair was often puzzled by the deposits in the long barrows they successfully dug, and disappointed by the lack of accompanying artifacts. They were likewise nonplussed by the positions of the bodies which Hoare recorded as 'strangely huddled', 'thrown promiscuously together', or 'lying in a confused and irregular manner'. Hoare usually noticed the ancient soils beneath long barrows, observing that the black loam forming the lower and middle parts of the mounds was a constant structural feature. He also recognised the dumped construction of some earthern long barrows raised by piling heaps along a selected axis. At Tilshead he wrote that 'the different strata bore the appearance of a circular barrow within the long one'.

Without realising it they recorded the remains of collapsed mortuary structures covering burials, and the remains of post-sockets holding timbers once supporting the roofs. At Boyton he described 'a pyramid of loose flints, marl, stone etc.' Beneath this pile were the burials, laid on the old ground surface beneath 'two excavations in the native soil, of an oval form and seven feet apart, which with the skeletons were covered with a pyramid of earth and stones'. The description clearly indicates the remnants of a timber building, perhaps stone-roofed, once protecting the bodies. Hoare felt the post-holes to be 'cists' and he occasionally describes the filling of these holes as 'vegetable mould', 'charred wood', 'wood ashes', etc. At Bowls Barrow was 'a ridge of large stones and flints, which extended wider as the men worked downward'. A 'floor of flints, regularly laid' had the burials placed on it. To Hoare the pile was in form 'like the ridge of a house'. Cunnington found a 'large cist' by the skeletons, again suggestive of a considerable post-hole. However, in common with many nineteenth-century archaeologists following in his footsteps, he did not equate the holes and collapsed debris with timbers and ritual structures. After digging into numerous long barrows Hoare was eventually forced to concede that 'notwithstanding our expensive and continued researches on them, we are obliged to confess our ignorance for what purpose they were originally constructed'. Later, in 1819, he deduced from the lack of gravegoods that 'they were appropriated to the lower class of people'.

Most of the Hoare-Cunnington excavation work, however, was carried out among the round-barrow cemeteries in Wiltshire, particularly those clustered around Stonehenge. Size was no deterrent, and probably the largest round barrow they attacked was the Hatfield Barrow, which was 22ft high. It has since been destroyed. The mound was composed of loose sand, and a shaft was sunk into the centre. This shaft progressively narrowed like an inverted cone the deeper they went, although 24ft of the old ground surface was exposed. Fortunately Cunnington saw the danger of working in such unstable material and withdrew the men shortly before part of the side fell in. Thus the labourers

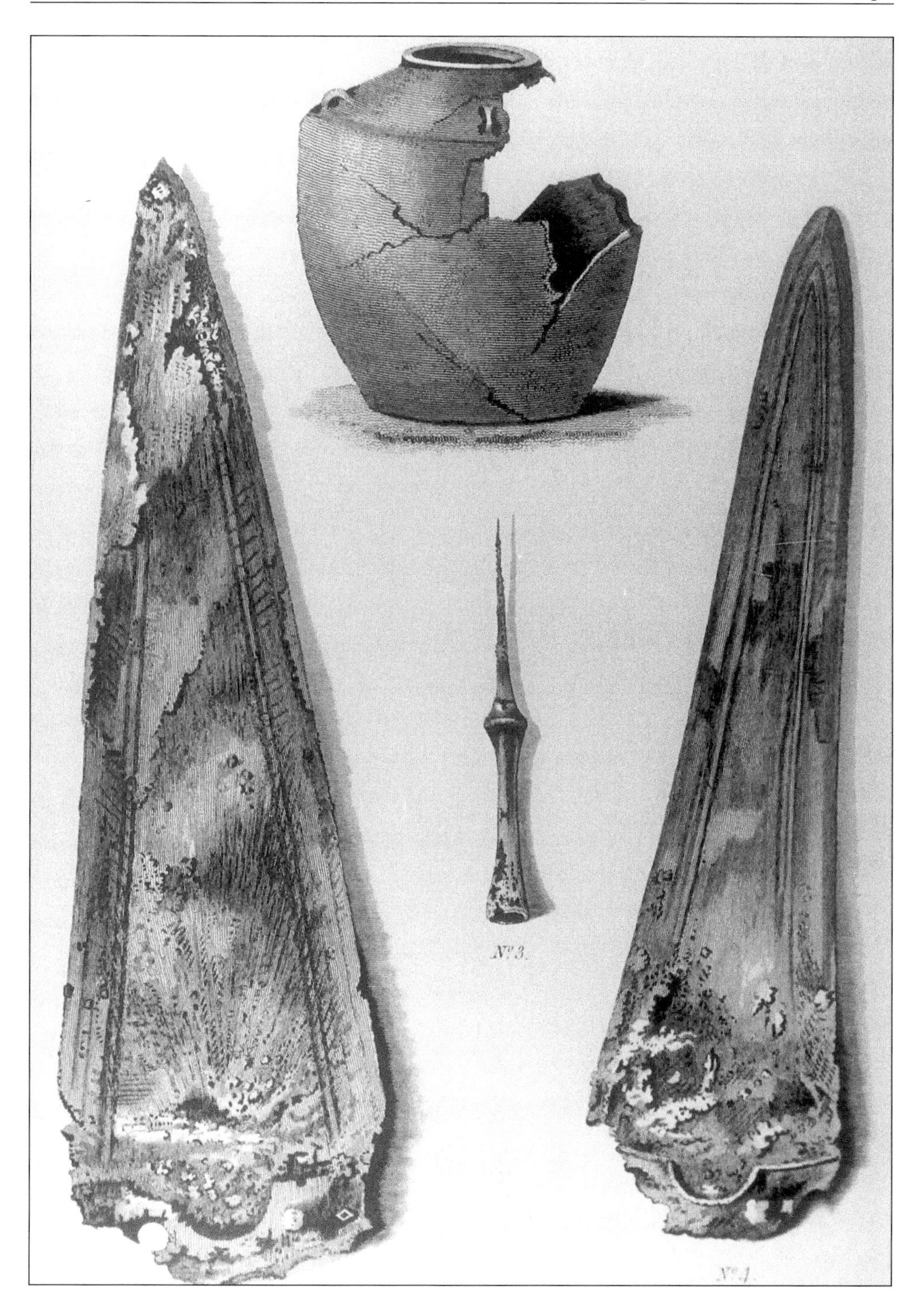

12 *Gravegoods from a bell barrow at Winterbourne Stoke, including two fine bronze daggers, pottery and a bronze awl, from a Crocker engraving. The remains of the leather sheaths can be clearly seen on the dagger blades.*

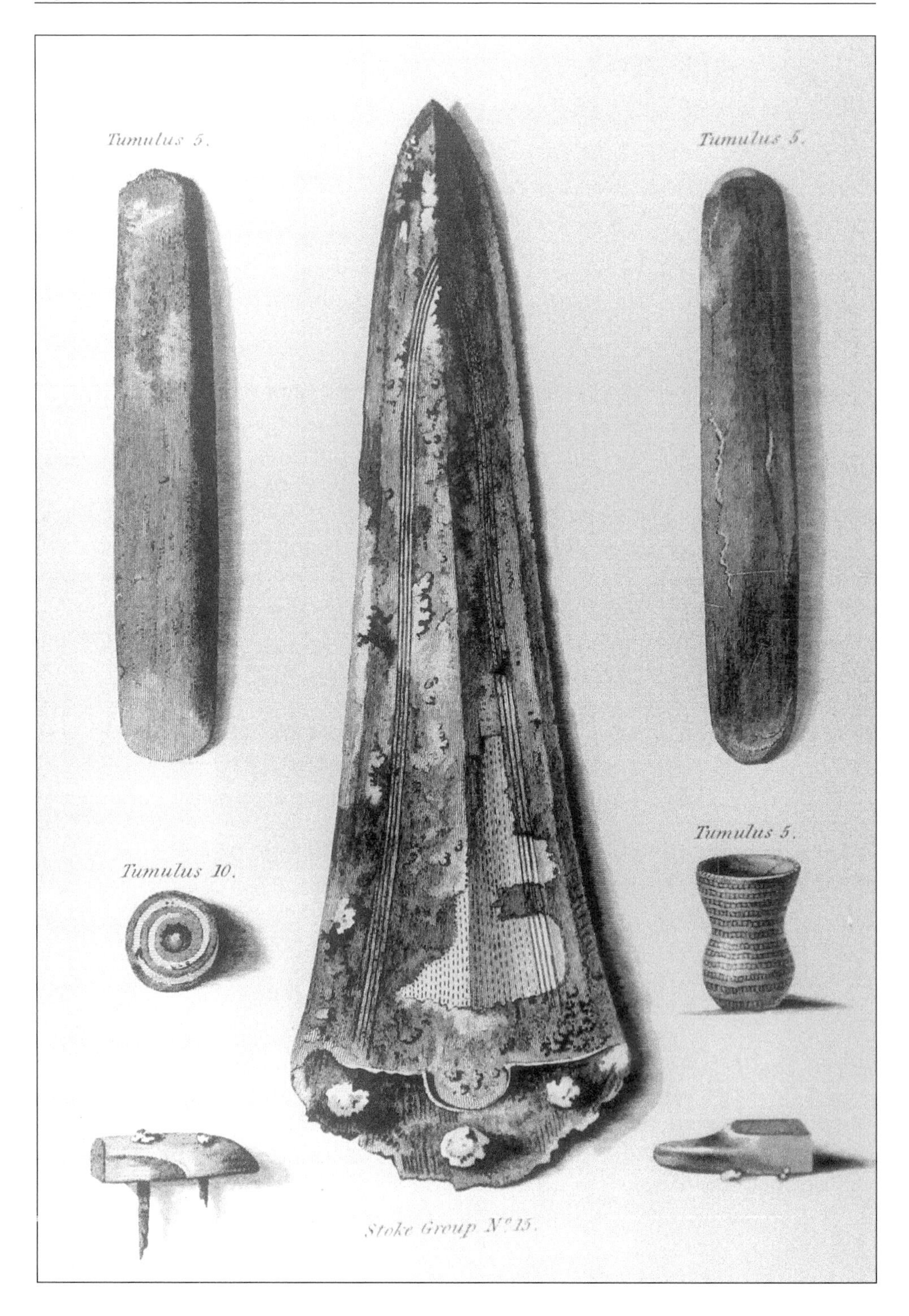

13 *Another fine engraving of finds from the same group, including another dagger, a pair of whetstones and a beaker.*

'most providentially escaped an untimely end'. Another dangerous adventure, with 'Gothick' overtones, occurred during the digging of a bell barrow on Oakley Down. To the excavation party it seemed that the gods disapproved of the unearthing of the skeleton, as a tremendous thunderstorm broke over their heads. Hoare remarked that the occasion 'will ever be remembered with horror and pleasure by those who were present'. The only refuge was the trench cut into the mound, but the lightning flashing on their spades and the flints cascading down on them from the barrow summit forced them to leave their shelter 'and abide the pelting of the pitiless storm upon the bleak and unsheltered down'. One of the party was so impressed by the occasion that he sent Hoare 'a beautiful and spirited poem' concerning the event, called 'Plaint of the Mighty Dead of Old', full of Romantic imagery.

Much backbreaking effort was also expended on a large barrow at Charnage Furze, near Deverill. Hoare wrote, 'we dug a great deal in this barrow, and I have still doubts whether we found the real and primary interment'. Hoare called another barrow near Kingston Deverill the 'Flint Barrow'. It was 76ft across and 13ft high. This huge mound was heavily assaulted and Hoare's labourers 'were obliged to throw out some fifty to one hundred loads of flints'. It must have been galling for him to learn, as he did later, that one side of the mound collapsed shortly after their departure, revealing three urns together near the surface. These were swiftly removed as trophies by the local peasantry and only a few urn sherds were recovered. Other barrows were evidently opened with far less trouble and expense. A group of diminutive ones near the Druid's Head Inn at Lake were explored 'in a leisure hour'. However, near Beckhampton Hoare once noticed 'a solitary barrow of low elevation' that promised little trouble. A feeling of disbelief is aroused when one reads his comment that 'this insignificant little mound' was expected to be plundered 'in a few minutes'. Actually it cost 'two hours time and a severe test of . . . curiosity and patience'!

Hoare's excavation parties apparently attracted spectators and doubtless some expeditions became social events patronised by the local aristocracy, antiquaries and others prompted by idle curiosity. Usually a week was set aside for a barrow-digging expedition; these were generally attended by a party of his companions, who usually lodged at Amesbury or Everley. Hoare comments on the attendance of 'many of my friends from Salisbury' on one occasion. On another, Cunnington, working among the Normanton group, 'was gratified with the presence of several learned and well-informed people on the scene of action'. At times Cunnington 'experienced a great deal of mortification on their account at our want of success'. Antiquaries who visited the diggings included several famous (or notorious) barrow openers such as Dean Merewether and the Reverend John Skinner. This pair watched the opening of a mound on Pound Down which prompted the latter to compose a lengthy, turgid poem called 'Beth Pennard, or the British Chieftain's Grave'. The work drags in Druids, bards, 'Verdant glades', 'ethereal sprites' and other Romantic trappings. Hoare gains mention as:

> . . . a kind chief, who will revere
> A chieftain's relics buried here.
> One who with us delights to ken
> The ancient works of Celtic men:

14 *Lead plaque and more sophisticated bronze disc left by Hoare in barrows dug by him. (Wiltshire Archaeological Museum)*

Thurnam reopened this barrow in the 1850s and found a metal disc, inscribed 'Opened by R.C.H.'. At Normanton a miniature cup with openwork sides was examined by 'an enthusiastic antiquary' who 'fancied that he could trace in this cup a design taken from the outward circle of Stonehenge'. The idea was certainly original! It seems certain that there was no lack of well-intentioned advice around when Hoare and Cunnington commenced their season's campaigns. Cunnington noted of the visitors, 'though they may not all of them be as sanguine barrow-hunters as the learned Baronet, yet they are all amateurs in such a degree as to relish the pursuit, and enjoy it'.

Cunnington's opening of the Bush Barrow in the Normanton group clearly shows the imperfect nature of their work, arousing feelings of horror when the account is closely read. The shovelling out of thousands of minute gold pins before they were noticed is bad enough, but the casual mention of a small dagger which evidently crumbled to pieces and was not recovered, and 'many small rings of bone' noticed but not preserved adds to the suspension of belief. A casual glance at the 1964 *Guide Catalogue* to the Devizes Museum collection reveals in concise form how much was not thought worthy of recovering or saving from the barrows, or indeed how much was collected and then subsequently lost.

Hoare and Cunnington worked together for the best part of six years, and after the latter's death Hoare pursued his investigations alone, although on a vastly reduced scale. Their collaboration marked the first serious attempt to investigate the origins of the prehistoric tumuli in any part of Britain, investigations strenuously pursued, faithfully written up and the finds preserved. Their investigations gave them the glimmering of the idea of a threefold classification of burials and artifacts into ages, an idea anticipated by Douglas, but only concisely expounded much later in the century. Indeed, Cunnington's *eminence grise*, Thomas Leman, wrote to the former:

15 'Group of Barrows, South of Stone Henge', a watercolour by Philip Crocker, Hoare's surveyor and draughtsman, c. 1806. The onlookers are Hoare and Cunnington, the diggers perhaps Stephen and John Parker. (Wiltshire Archaeological Museum)

> I think we distinguish three great eras by the arms of offence found in our barrows. Ist those of bone and stone, certainly belonging to the primeval inhabitants in their savage state, and which may safely be attributed to the Celts. 2nd those of brass probably imported into this island from the more polished nations of Africa in exchange for our tin, and which may be given to the Belgae. 3rd those of iron, introduced but a little while before the invasion of the Romans.

Sadly no mention of this idea was committed to the pages of *Ancient Wiltshire*, and it was 30 years before Thomsen was to argue this basic chronological distinction in print in Denmark.

As far as the ceremonies relating to the erection of barrows were concerned, Hoare realised in the second volume of his great history that 'though further exploration might add new articles to our museum, it would not probably procure much additional information respecting the funeral rites of the Britons'. Hence the collection of mere finds was not the main reason for his vast ranging operations. Hoare's collection, incidentally, fortunately remains more or less intact. Preserved at Stourhead after his death, it suffered some neglect. In the cellars there it appeared 'to unarchaeological eyes more like the refuse of a marine store than anything else'. Fortunately it was deposited on loan in the Wiltshire Archaeological Society's Museum at Devizes in 1878, and was purchased outright in 1883

16 *Articles from Bush Barrow, including a gold scabbard hook, a fossil pebble macehead and part of a rotted wooden dagger handle inlaid with tiny gold nails in a chevron pattern. All the above engravings are figured in* Ancient Wiltshire.

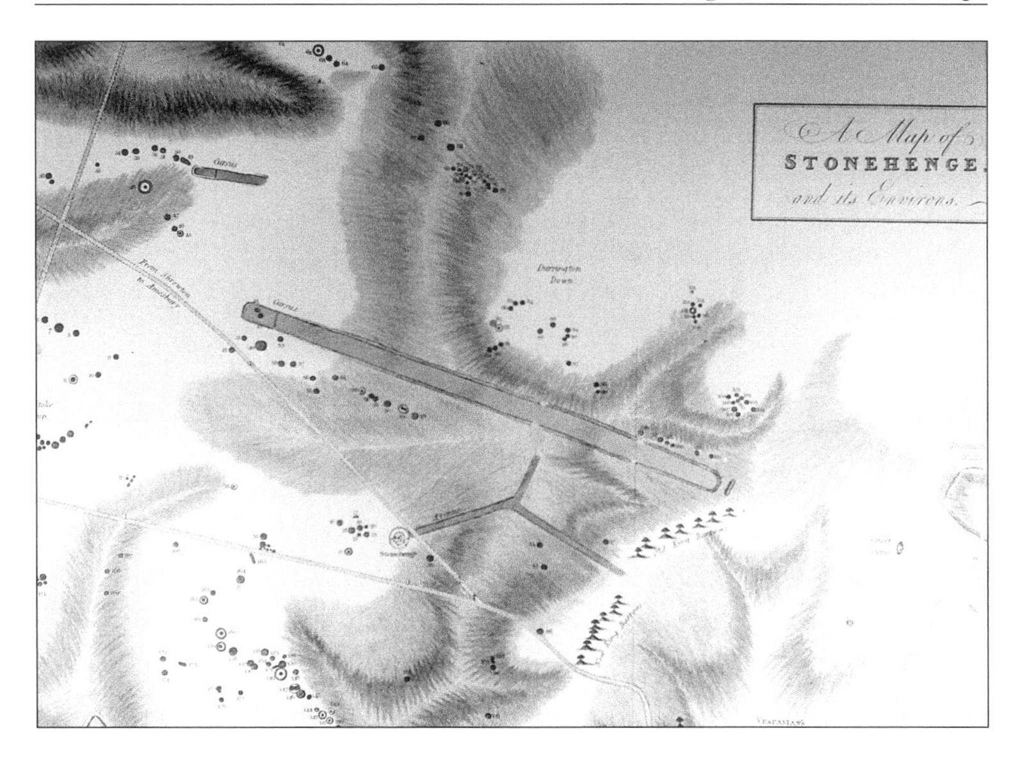

17 *Large-scale map of the Stonehenge area drawn by Crocker identifying all the barrows dug by Hoare and Cunnington. Their sites are numbered and can be looked up in the text of* Ancient Wiltshire. *The map was an innovation ignored by subsequent large-scale barrow openers for nearly a century.*

for £250 by the Trustees of the Society — i.e. for only £50 more than Hoare had originally given for it.

Hoare and Cunnington had a genuine thirst for antiquarian knowledge based on thorough field research. They stand as pioneers, innovators, who laid the basis for all that was to follow. Whatever their faults — and they were those of the times — British archaeology owes them a vast debt. It was indeed fortunate that they joined forces, bequeathing to posterity a classic of antiquarian literature and a collection of prehistoric material 'whose content', as the *Guide Catalogue* puts it, 'has such a cardinal significance for Bronze Age archaeology'.

4 Author-antiquaries, and others

Barrow digging seems clearly to have gained its impetus from the work of Hoare and Cunnington. The early nineteenth century saw the real beginning of barrow opening on a large scale; much of it was careless and indiscriminate, faults that were to last throughout the century and beyond. The period ushered in the age of the dilettante, usually of the gentleman class, whose employees plundered mounds wholesale in the search for curios to fill showcases and cabinets. Rarely, if ever, were the results of their plunderings recorded, and thus much valuable information was lost to posterity. By the middle of the century a number of authorities were condemning the wholesale desecration wrought on burial mounds in the name of mere 'treasure-hunting'. Indiscriminate digging is a subject that will be returned to time and again in this work.

There were a number of excavators enlightened enough to dig for the sake of interest and knowledge in England in the early 1800s, and their work will be examined in the appropriate chapters. However, most of these early enthusiasts performed in a regrettably casual manner, as at the opening of the Great Barrow at Stow Heath, Aylsham, Norfolk, in 1808. The mound, 30 yards across and 12ft high, was opened by means of 'a hole . . . about four yards wide and two yards deep'. Nothing was found until 'on shoving down the sides to fill up the cavity ... a curious Urn was discovered, which was cut through the middle by a spade'. A sketch of the pot was swiftly made before it was 'quite destroyed, it being too soft a substance to be taken up in large fragments'. Doubtless this type of excavation had its parallels elsewhere, not all committed, as this one was, to the pages of *Archaeologia* or kindred journals.

An interesting excavation on a barrow at Beedon in Berkshire was carried out in 1815, though not published till the 1850s. The diggers had great difficulty in securing permission to excavate, as the tenant and his wife feared that any opening of the mound would raise the ghosts of those interred there. However, 'the promise that all valuables discovered should be rendered up to them, at length secured their permission'. The excavation was thus commenced. However:

> The work was much impeded . . . by a violent thunderstorm, which the country people regarded as in some manner caused by the sacrilegious undertaking to disturb the dead. One of the labourers employed left the work in consequence, and much alarm prevailed.

The opening, in fact, revealed some form of wooden stake circle or allied timber structure, the first ever noticed in British barrow archaeology. The account stated that:

> A regular horizontal layer of charred wood appeared, placed on a stratum of red clay . . . (the old ground surface?). The workmen found seven perpendicular holes, formed almost in a circle, around the centre of the barrow. They were about a foot in depth, and two inches in diameter, and were partly filled with charred wood.

Despite its early date, this barrow opening appears to have been conducted by an enlightened group of antiquaries.

One of the much-maligned diggers of the early nineteenth century was the Reverend John Skinner (1772–1839). A friend of Hoare, he opened some 26 barrows in Somerset between 1815 and 1818, around his Camerton parish. He wrote up the details of his perambulations and researches in England and elsewhere in 98 manuscript volumes, profusely illustrated with watercolour drawings. These were bequeathed to the British Museum on condition that they were not opened for 50 years. These record his perambulatory researches throughout Britain, and are replete with agonizing details of the shortcomings of his delvings, with references to pickaxed urns broken by clumsy and often unsupervised workmen, and sites trampled by the hoofs of flocks of straying sheep. Skinner was a Fellow of the Society of Antiquaries and was interested in etymology as well as archaeology. As an archaeologist his work was painfully crude, even by the low standards then obtaining. On one single afternoon for instance, he, or rather his labourers, dug into no less than six barrows. He described in casual fashion that nothing was found since his men 'missed the centre, or did not dig deep enough'! On another occasion he remarked that four barrows were dug without result, but the labourers did their work so badly that they may have 'digged wide of the cists as he was not on the spot to direct them, and could not rectify his mistake except by working the ground all over again'!

In 1816 Skinner, acting on behalf of Hoare, dug into the chambered long barrow at Stoney Littleton. In his account of the excavation, Hoare describes that under Skinner's 'judicious and able guidance, an opening was made in the roof.' In other words, one of the finest examples of a transepted gallery grave in Britain was entered via a gap forced between two of the capstones. Skinner afterwards remarked that the mound 'was never properly examined until I had done it'!

An amusing and rather sad little story about Skinner concerns some amber beads found by him with a cremation in a group of tumuli called the 'Priddy Nine Barrows'. The beads were of a rich ruby colour, and to his pleasure Skinner found that one of them contained a bee which had been trapped in the resin when it was still fluid. One day he was showing this prize of his collection to a Mrs Raisbeck, when the unfortunate lady let it slip from her fingers. It fell on to an iron chest, and shattered. Skinner was most upset, although he did his best not to show it, but poor Mrs Raisbeck was inconsolable, as the object was, as she put it, irreplaceable. When she left the Parsonage, she was still distraught. Skinner gallantly attempted to ease her feelings by dashing off a few lines of verse on the subject, and sending them to her by messenger. Unfortunately she did not receive them. This was a pity since they possess some little charm and are worth repeating. Skinner titled it 'Lines written on the escape of a bee from his imprisonment of 2,000 years, to a fair lady who was the fortunate cause of this emancipation. January 24th 1826.'

> Escaped at length our Druid's bee
> Fulfils his mystic destiny
> Which dooms whatever is to be.
> How sweet his freedom we suppose
> When his deliverer is a Rose
> With looks so sweet and bloom so fair.
> Oh! Like this bee be mine the doom
> That Angels greet me from the tomb
> Then my imprisonment will seem
> Tho' thrice his time a moment's dream.

Skinner's end was unfortunate. In 1839 in the 67th year of his life, he shot himself in a wood, after a quarrel with his sons and daughter.

During the period from 1826 to 1845 three small privately printed literary works appeared, dealing with aspects of barrows and barrow digging. One of them, *Barrow Digging by a Barrow-Knight* (1845) deals with Bateman's operations and will be described later. The others were *The Deverel Barrow* (1826) and *The Barrow Diggers* (1839). The former was written by William Augustus Miles in commemoration of the opening of a barrow the previous year. He comments presciently in the text that 'In the absence of History, the spade is no mean historian'. The work is a rather dramatised account, and describes the finding of numerous urn cremations in the mound in question. Not surprisingly in view of the antiquarian climate of the day, the author emerges as an incipient druidophile, with his references to 'the soothsayers, as they marked the trickling course of human blood ... invoked in all their wild and imposing gore-drenched ceremonies, the vengeance of the gods upon their foes' and to 'the war-exciting and despotic Druids'. In one purple passage the author pictures the scene of the work as evening closed in on the Dorset downland:

> In some cases, when night was stealing on and an urn had been partially discovered, in order to ensure its preservation, I have bivouacked round the fire with my labourers 'til near midnight, no pleasant situation on a bleak and elevated Dorset down on a November night. Men were employed in dragging furze from an adjoining spot and it was a fine subject for the talent of an artist to have described the venerable Urn smoking at the flame, while a red and flickering gleam played upon the countenances of the labourers, who speaking in low and subdued tones, and having their eyes fixed upon the flames and dead men's bones were afraid to look into the surrounding darkness. The swell of the passing breeze as it fanned the fire raised them from their reverie, or roused their attention from some direful story of goblin damned, which was gravely related and as faithfully believed. The effect produced by the narrative of the village thatcher added most strongly to the horror of their situation as he gravely declared that his father and elder brother had been most cruelly dragged about and beaten by some invisible hand on the very down on which we stood. There was no danger of a Deserter from my party, as fear kept them together, and our

> group was augmented by the curiosity of the passing peasants, who deviating from their homeward course wondered why a fire blazed on the unfrequented Down, a spot which it is more than probable no fire had gleamed since the last Deposit was pompously and religiously placed in the Barrow just explored, save at the May-eve rites. But now how changed the scene. The Urn when it was last seen by man, so hallowed, so venerated, the form, the features of the chief whose ashes it contained, fresh to the minds and perhaps dear to the memories of those who assisted at the sepulchral ceremonies, now after the lapse of many hundred years, calmly reeked before a burning faggot to the rude gaze of an astonished peasant.

Hoare, who wrote the introduction to the work, felt the barrow had been raised for a family deposit. Two large stones in the barrow were in his opinion altars. He also thought that the mound must have been frequently reopened to receive further burial deposits. The burial mound itself was opened by a section 6ft wide from near the extreme edge, 'making a passage to the centre'. Distressed by the clumsiness of his labourers, which resulted in the smashing of some of the encisted urns, Miles worked out a system in his 'subsequent proceedings' to avoid similar accidents. His eventual method was to remove 'the bed of native chalk till parallel with the cist; then by striking a passage through, I was enabled to extract the urn without displacing the stones, which for many ages had remained undisturbed'. Incidentally the fires blazing around the barrow were to 'evaporate the moisture from the pottery'. Many of the cists and their contents were damp and had to be dried out before the urns could be safely removed. Today this famous barrow still exists, tree-covered and surrounded by a wall of flints.

The other work, also featuring digging in Dorset, was written anonymously by the Reverend Charles Woolls to mark the 'exceedingly agreeable' opening of the Shapwick Barrow in the parish of Sturminster Marshall. The text imitates the dialogue between Hamlet and the gravedigger in Shakespeare's tragedy. The book's importance lies in the profuse explanatory notes which contain much useful information regarding Dorset antiquities. The notes were written:

> with the desire of recalling to the remembrance of Barrow Diggers the principal characteristics of their subterranean pursuits, and directing the attention of the curious Inquirer to almost the only source from whence any information can be derived of the Manners and Customs of the early Inhabitants of Britain.

The text of the *Diggers* illustrates the ideas and methods of the openers, voiced in the song of the First Barrow Digger:

> Clasps, Celts and arrow-heads, I'll try
> To claw within my Clutch,
> And if a Shield I should espy,
> I'll vow there ne'er was such.

> With Popish Tricks, and Relics rare.
> The Priests their Flocks do gull,
> In casting out the earth take care,
> Huzza! I've found a skull.

Primitive advice on digging equipment specified that:

> A Mattoc, Shovel, and a Spade,
> Will dig up human bones.'

Woolls's notes explained how barrows should be opened according to the methods then appertaining. He states that:

> the way to open a barrow, is either to remove the mound of earth entirely, or to make a section through it at least six or eight feet wide from north to south, or from east to west, or sink a shaft down the centre from top to bottom. Sir R.C. Hoare invariably adhered to the latter mode with a desire not to injure the external form. The greatest caution should be used in removing the earth, especially when charcoal and fragments of pottery appear intermingled with it; for it not unfrequently happens that relics or interments are found near the surface, or round the outside of a Barrow. With respect to the Deposits, Mr Cunnington first discovered and established contrary to the theory of Dr Stukeley, that the primary interment is always on the floor of a Barrow or in a cist dug in the chalk beneath it . . . when a wall or heap of flints closely arranged together present themselves, they should be removed with the hand, because a pick-axe, crow-bar, or spade at such a crisis has often destroyed an Urn, by making an irruption into the cist. On arriving at the cist, the operations should be conducted slowly around its edge either with a trowel or a knife. Want of success at first should never terminate in abandoning a Barrow until it has been thoroughly examined.

One of the plates in the book shows the barrow during the course of the excavations. The mound, standing 10ft high on a level plain, was penetrated by a roughly hewn gash 8ft wide, driven 46ft through the centre to the other side. A shaft was then sunk below the old ground surface in the centre, its floor reached via a ladder. This shaft was abandoned when the water table was encountered. The whole undertaking lasted eight days, then a considerable period of time for such an operation.

During the same decade William Crawford Williamson (1816–95), published a pamphlet entitled *Description of the Tumulus opened at Gristhorpe near Scarborough* (1834). The author, a precocious young man of 17, later achieved eminence as Professor of Natural History at Manchester University, and could be said to be one of the founders of palaeobotany. The barrow contained a skeleton laid in a lidded oak trunk coffin, which owed its preservation to the water-holding nature of the boulder clay of Gristhorpe cliff. The body had been wrapped in animal skin, and the bones stained ebony by the tannic

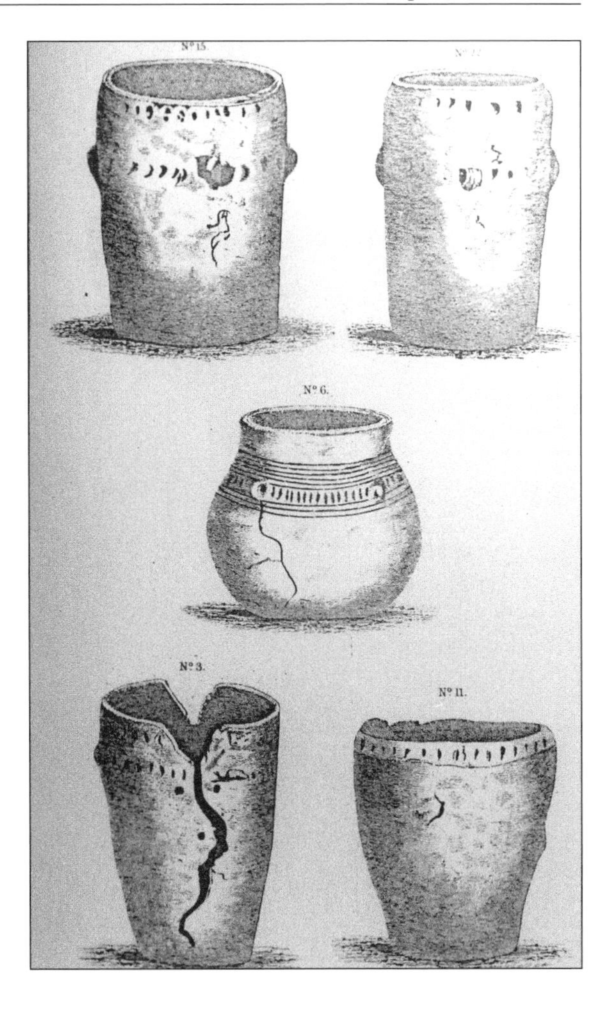

18 *Urns recovered from the Deverel Barrow by William Miles, and illustrated in his book of the same name (1826).*

acid in the oak. In association were a flint 'javelin', two flint arrowheads, a bronze or copper dagger with a bone pommel, a bone pin and a wickerwork basket, all carefully illustrated in the published account. A quantity of vegetable substances was also found within the coffin, originally described as the remains of mistletoe. In the oft-repeated phrase of the time they soon 'crumbled into dust'.

The rather decayed bones of the skeleton were stabilised, in an early example of conservation, by being boiled in gelatine. This early Yorkshireman, together with his coffin and relics, is still one of the sights of the Rotunda Museum in Scarborough. In fact the dig itself taught an important lesson, not appreciated until that time, that it was possible to construct a detailed picture of early man, in favourable circumstances, by a careful consideration of the material survivals.

The growing interest in archaeology was reflected in the founding in 1843 of the 'British Archaeological Association for the Encouragement and Prosecution of Researches into the Arts and Monuments of the Early Middle Ages'. Its 1,200 members comprised a wide cross-section of early Victorian society. The association inaugurated a series of

19 *Opening of the Shapwick Barrow (1838), from Charles Woolls's* The Barrow Diggers. *Note the wide trench hewed through the mound and the ladder descending into the pit below the old ground surface.*

summer meetings, the first being the celebrated Canterbury Congress of 1844, the earliest archaeological conference on record. The congress included such diverse entertainment as tours through the cathedral; a display of the municipal archives, and archaeological objects, including Faussett's great collection of Saxon antiquities; the unwrapping of an Egyptian mummy; and the opening of certain Saxon barrows on Breach Downs. These openings (eight of them in one day) were supervised by Lord Albert Conyngham, afterwards Lord Londesborough. The work was witnessed by some 200 guests who flocked to the Downs in a procession of private carriages and hired vehicles. Labourers had already lowered the mounds to within two feet of the presumed position of the burials, and his lordship, 'dressed in an exploring costume', merely superintended the uncovering of the skeletons. The operations were constantly interrupted by drenching downpours, necessitating the frequent use of umbrellas. The fair sex were well represented among the gathering, the local press noting that ladies 'crowded round the tumuli and almost passionately expressed their gratification as beads, and the wire on which they were strung, or amulet, or ring or armlet was handed to them for inspection.' Likewise the 'juvenile peasantry' showed great curiosity in the proceedings 'as eagerly poring after relics as any Archaeologist present'. The Reverend Stephen Isaacson, later responsible for the poetic dissertation on Bateman's 'opening parties', was present at Canterbury, and he scribbled some verses describing the activities during the excavations:

20 *The skeleton and massive oak trunk coffin dug out of the clifftop barrow at Gristhorpe near Scarborough in 1834, an early example of the survival of organic remains preserved by waterlogging. (Scarborough Museum)*

21 *Drenched members of the British Archaeological Association surveying the dampish barrow diggings on Breach Downs, Kent, in September 1844, one of the activities organised for the first Congress of the BAA at Canterbury.*

This is the scud, that took place in the mud,
While we sat and looked on from the carriage;
Such a dash was not seen, such a splash has not been,
My dear Bob, since the day of my marriage.

Fine ladies so soiled, as onward they toiled,
While Professors so grave grubbed away;
Would have made you declare, had you only been there,
It was ten times as good as a play.

Such dragging of skirts! such giggling of flirts,
As you see in a storm on Hyde Park;
With no end of umbrellas to shelter the Fellows,
Who seemed bent on digging till dark.

Sir William Beetham, of course too was with 'em,
Its nothing without 'Ulster King',
How he handled the thigh-bones, and other queer dry bones,
Sometimes shouting out — 'No such thing !'

Then the chuckles o'er buckles, as down on their knuckles,
They picked up little odd bits of brass;
The clowns standing round, asking what they had found,
If coins? and they thought they would pass.

During the Breach Down diggings, Professor Buckland attempted to trick Lord Conyngham's servant, Charles, who was working in one of the barrows. He pulled a ring off his finger and pushed it into the ground close to where Charles was carefully scraping. Charles eventually uncovered the ring, and after a cursory glance flicked it on to the spoil heap with his trowel point. 'What's that?' quoth the Professor. 'Oh, 'twon't do for me,' was the reply. 'Well, but it's a ring I've picked up.' 'Yes, but you put it there first.' Evidently Charles was not as gullible as he may have appeared! In a letter written shortly after the Congress to Albert Way, John Henry Parker (who had admitted having 'some sleep' during the mummy unwrapping), noted that 'the Canterbury Meeting has gone off brilliantly ...' Among other matters he informed his correspondent that 'the ransackers of the graves of their ancestors were very pleased with the results of their proceedings.' Indeed it seems that this first ever Association field week impressed most of those who had attended. Among them was Thomas Bateman of Middeton-by-Youlgrave, Derbyshire. Charles Roach Smith wrote of Bateman in his *Retrospections* that 'the Canterbury Congress introduced him to the world'.

5 Peakland pioneers

In the final note to his *Barrow Digging by a Barrow-Knight*, recounting his Derbyshire sojourn, the Reverend Stephen Isaacson wrote:

> A worthy fellow-labourer (to Hoare) has sprung up in this hitherto neglected quarter of England, qualified in every respect to rescue from oblivion her buried treasures, and restore her to the position to which she is entitled, amongst the important locations of the earliest settlers of this island, in the person of *Thomas Bateman, Jun., Esq.*, in whose labours we have been permitted to participate, and in whose success we rejoice.

Bateman stands high among the 'big four' nineteenth-century, prehistoric barrow-diggers, a group which also includes Hoare, Greenwell and Mortimer. He was, by the magnitude of his operations, the real successor to the first, to whose opinions in part he defers, and whose terminology he adopts. Bateman also followed the traditions established by those of his fellow countymen who had gone before — Dr Samuel Pegge, Major Hayman Rooke, Samuel Mitchell, and his own father William Bateman. Pegge, White Watson and Rooke were among the earliest to dig into the rich collection of Peak District burial mounds (henceforward referred to as 'cairns' since they were almost all constructed of piles of heaped-up stones). Samuel Pegge (1704–96), a cleric from Chesterfield, who lived to an advanced age, was amongst the earliest investigators to probe the cairns of the Derbyshire Peak, communicating the results of his discoveries to *Archaeologia* and the *Gentleman's Magazine*. He added practical experience to offset mere conjecture, produced plans of his sites and sketches of his finds. His 'Disquisition into the Lows of the High Peak' in *Archaeologia* V11 was the first to attempt a discussion on the distribution, form and purpose of the Derbyshire tumuli. Oxford University recognised the importance of his contributions in many spheres by creating him Ll.D in 1791.

As early as 1782 Hayman Rooke (1723–1806) had driven two sections across the huge cairn built into the bank of the Arbor Low henge monument, an undertaking that took five days — an almost unheard-of length of time for a barrow dig in the eighteenth century. This cairn, and nearby Gib Hill, had, because of their proximity to Arbor Low, an almost magnetic attraction for early Derbyshire antiquarians until Bateman solved their secrets in the 1840s. Rooke himself, nicknamed the 'Resurrection Major' by the local gentry, dug at a number of other sites, and the results of his work, and his field observations, can be read in early issues of *Archaeologia*, or in his neat precise field sketchbooks in Sheffield Museum. Some of his contributions appear in Douglas's great work. They show an acute perception and precision in description and illustration, but, not surprisingly perhaps, his ideas fly fancifully through realms peopled by Druids, bards and priests. Yet mixed with this wild fantasy are solid and important observations, some dealing with monuments now long since destroyed. In fact Rooke corresponded regularly with Douglas, who wrote to the former in January 1787:

> I have a strong *presentiment* that Derbyshire from its mountainous, and in some respects uncultivated state, contains many extraordinary fine undiscribed and unexplored remains of very antient places of sepulchre.

Rooke's antiquarian susceptibilities were occasionally imposed upon. Once he dug into a cairn called Abbot's Low, uncovering an urn cremation first found by the local landowner and reportedly covered by a flat stone. The stone was carved with an inscription which read *Gell Prae CIII LV Brit.* Rooke was persuaded that this indicated the urn held a Roman interment, and that the cremated bones were those of a remote relative of the Gells, one Gellius, owners of the land on which the cairn stood! Rooke published the details of the dig in *Archaeologia*. The general feeling was that the inscription had been 'planted', and the cynical rejoinder was that 'a Gell had transformed a Rooke into a gull'.

White Watson of Bakewell employed one Francis Walker to 'get urns' from some mounds in the cairn cemetery on Stanton Moor, but no written information on these has survived. The next workers in the field were William Bateman (1787–1835), a rich and leisured Derbyshire country gentleman, and Samuel Mitchell (1803–65), a Sheffield solicitor. Mitchell, then a young man, made the acquaintance of Bateman in the early 1820s. Mitchell had a strong predilection for archaeology, and it is doubtless this common bond which brought the pair in contact. The Reverend Joseph Hunter referred to him as 'a young and zealous antiquary'. The account of their joint investigations was later written up and published by Thomas Bateman, William's son, but for some reason Mitchell's part in the operations was ignored. It is difficult to account for this, but it was one of Bateman's failings that he sometimes neglected to give credit to his co-workers. The omission of Mitchell's name was unfortunate, since he wrote his own accounts of the diggings in one of the volumes of his *Memoranda* (now in the British Museum). From these it would appear that he was a keen and enthusiastic researcher, interested in excavation for its own sake, while William Bateman is known rather as a collector of the dilettante order. The latter comment, however, might be a disservice to Bateman's own known archaeological enthusiasm.

From his writings it seems that Mitchell's technique was to drive trenches to the centre of the cairns he dug, from some point on the circumference. The work was hasty, but according to the tenets then prevailing. On one day several small cairns near the Carl Wark hillfort were attacked with negative results. On another occasion a cairn in Haddon Fields yielded 70 intrusive Roman copper coins; the finds persuaded Mitchell that the mound 'was constructed in the reign of Emperor Gratian'. He consistently favoured a Roman date for the prehistoric cairns he and Bateman opened. Of mounds opened by the pair near Youlgrave, he writes, 'I am decidedly of the opinion that they are all Roman or Romanised British.' The works of Hoare were evidently not known to Mitchell, hence the former's incense cups appeared to the latter to be 'earthen lamps'. Cinerary urns were invariably 'sun-baked', and a bronze awl was a 'copper pin . . . which had previously served as a fastening for the dress'.

Mitchell's accounts of his work only concern the period 1824 to 1826, although his writings indicate that he first dug at least as early as 1818, and worked with Bateman from 1821 onwards. (He was still digging as late as 1850). In his writings he often carefully noted the structure of mounds (which Hoare rarely did). Hence the Gib Hill cairn was reported to consist of 'loose stones and earth', for two yards, a thin layer of 'tuft-stone', a yard and a half of further stones and earth, a second 'tuft-stone' stratum, then one and a half yards of stiff red-brown clay mixed with charcoal ('marks of fire'). 'This clay was laid on the natural soil . . . and was throughout its whole circumference full of burnt bones and charcoal, disposed apparently in layers.' A further stratum of tuft-stone was placed below this; it had been changed into a 'yellow ochry substance by the action of fire'. Below this was solid rock. Mitchell sought a specialist report on the 'red-brown' clay, submitting it to Sir Francis Darwin and Dr Booth. Here he followed in the path of Hoare who successfully sought identification of a large animal bone found in a barrow, by showing it to his butcher! William Bateman asked Cunnington's friend the Reverend Thomas Leman to examine finds from the Kenslow cairn. He also sought a phrenological report from Dr Hibbert of Manchester on a skull from the same mound.

William Bateman's son Thomas (1821–61) was born in 1821. Bereft of his mother very early in life, he received a home education, before attending the Reverend Fearon's Academy at Bootle; back home he was soon steeped in antiquarian lore. His father died in 1835 when Thomas was 14. He was then brought up by his grandfather, Thomas Bateman Esq., of Middleton Hall, High Sheriff of Derbyshire in 1823. On Thomas senior's death in 1847, his vast estates devolved on his grandson. These riches he inherited enabled him to build up a huge library and museum of which his own archaeological collection was only a part. Bateman's main fame is based on his work on burial mounds, of which he or his lieutenants dug some 400 in Derbyshire, Staffordshire and the East and North Ridings of Yorkshire. He and his co-workers were among the most prolific excavators in the field of English prehistory. Although his work was somewhat hurried and lacking in care, it was better than that carried out by most other workers of the time, and the results were always carefully written up.

Bateman had a deep fondness for archaeological research; as he said in his first book *Vestiges of the Antiquities of Derbyshire* (1848), 'an early predilection for archaeological pursuits called him forth to many pleasurable excursions'. He remarked that his 'journeys in search of the antique have afforded the happiest portion of his career', and that his book was enlarged from his journal, 'more by the pleasure of revisiting in fancy scenes of past enjoyment, and by a wish to communicate any facts that might be made available for the diffusion of antiquarian science, than by any motives of mercenary or ambitious character'.

The possession of a considerable fortune gave Bateman the necessary leisure to pursue his activities. At first he directed the excavations in his native county and in neighbouring Staffordshire, but from the spring of 1845 Samuel Carrington, a village schoolmaster from Wetton in that county took over operations there. From 1849 James Ruddock, taxidermist, dug into certain Yorkshire tumuli chiefly around Pickering and later Whitby,

22 *The Reverend Samuel Pegge (1704–96), cleric and antiquary who opened burial mounds in his native Derbyshire, and wrote some of the earliest commentaries on the cairns of the Peak.*

on Bateman's behalf. Other barrow-digging helpers of an amateur status included Thomas Nadauld Brushfield (1829–1910), a protege of Bateman, and later, like Thurnam whom he knew well, superintendent of a mental asylum, and William Bowman (1829–58), a York artist, racy, somewhat indolent, but at his best a gifted painter (having studied under Etty).

Bateman's working parties usually numbered three or four. Among them his brother-in-law, William Parker, was prominent. A sketch of him appears in a vignette opposite the introduction to *Vestiges*, where he is described as a 'distinguished barrow-opener'. A glimpse of Bateman's early operations appears in Isaacson's *Barrow Digging by a Barrow-Knight*. The Reverend Stephen Isaacson (1798–1849) met Bateman at the Canterbury Congress and afterwards visited him at Lomberdale House. He accompanied Bateman on a number of digs and as a result wrote his humorous literary curiosity in 'six fyttes with notes by an Esquire', describing a typical excursion. The frontispiece illustrates an actual opening, of Taylor's Low, Wetton, in 1845. The legend 'was written for a friendly few'. It contains a mine of useful information on the personalities, techniques and general *modus operandi* of a typical Bateman expedition. In the body of the work Bateman is 'the Leader', whose:

> eyes upon the barrow bent are
> As if they'd pierce earth's very centre.

Parker is shown as an ardent enthusiast, vigorous in the pursuit of relics:

Naught would have better suited Parker
In these pursuits a very Fakir.
In fact I very little doubt
He'd beat the Eastern out and out!

Carrington is noted in a brief, anonymous couplet:

And would our time or space afford,
We'd tell of school-master abroad.

Isaacson also mentions himself, intimating that his function was more that of observer than performer:

But who's he armed with shining trowel,
Who all their labours watches so well?
If fond of work he does not shew it—
Why! that's the barrow-diggers' poet.

Even Bateman's dog is introduced in an atrocious punning piece of versification:

Besides old Nutt of dogs the colonel
Does not our special notice earn ill,—
For he delights at us to stare
As if, instead of skull, 'twas hare
We sought in antiquated lowe;

The excavation equipment is listed:

. . . bring the barrow tools,
Pick, shovel, scratcher, trowel, rules

and some good advice is offered on methods of procedure when interments were in close proximity:

. . . hither bring my trusty scratcher,
'Mongst barrow-tools there's none to match her,
And tread not heavily, because it
May seriously affect deposit,
For Briton's skull so long in ground
Is very seldom perfect found;
And what we scarcely deem a less ill
You may destroy a potter's vessel,
Which formed of potter's clay, though thick,
Can scarce withstand the blow of pick!

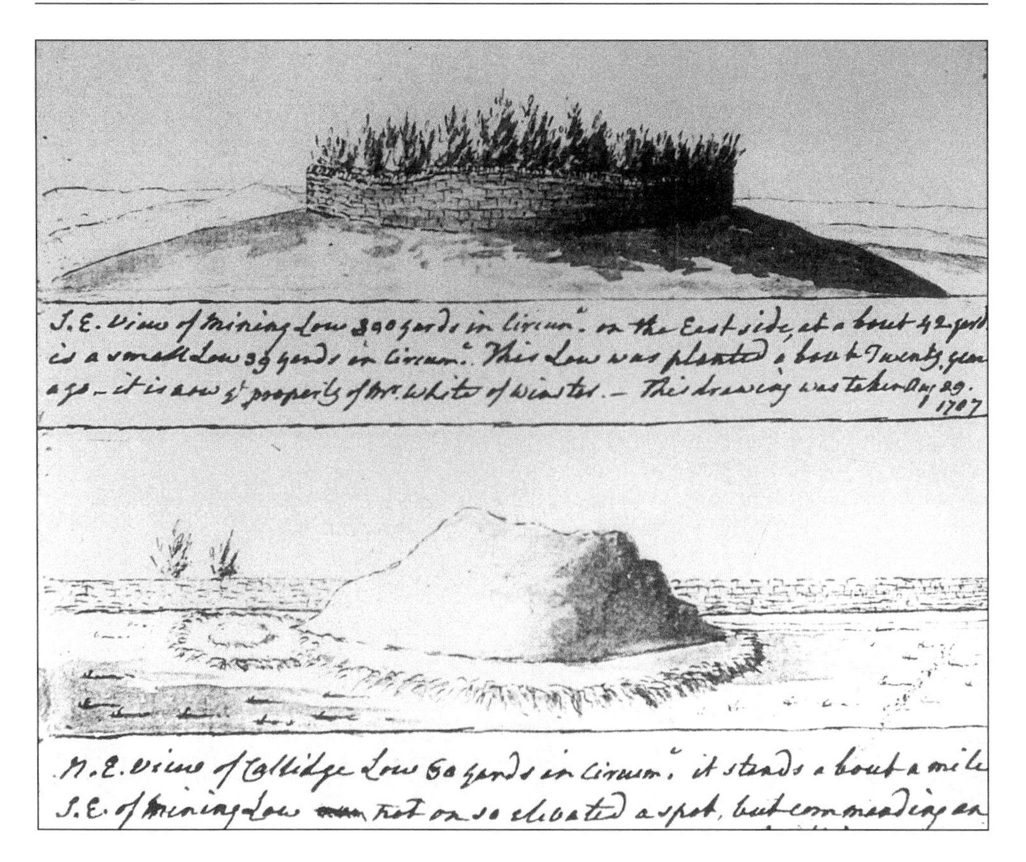

23 *Sketches by Hayman Rooke (1723–1806), showing Peak District cairns discovered by him on his archaeological rambles. The 'Resurrection Major' dug into a number of barrows, and drew plans of cemeteries and gravegoods later published in* Archaeologia.

The provision of adequate supplies of liquid and solid refreshment is mentioned more than once by Isaacson. Early in the first fytte he comments on the culinary preparations for the excavation party:

> So ham, veal, rabbits, lamb, at once were thrust,
> With varied condiments beneath a crust.

At midday a truly gargantuan feast was swiftly demolished:

> Pie of rabbits-tongue-and chine—
> Leg of poultry-cheek of swine—
> Pickled salmon-onion-mango—
> Down the throat fast as they can go.
> Brandy and beer
> Bring up the rear.

24 *Gravegoods, including an urn, miniature cup and jet pendant, discovered by Rooke in a mound on Stanton Moor, Derbyshire, and published in* Archaeologia *in 1784.*

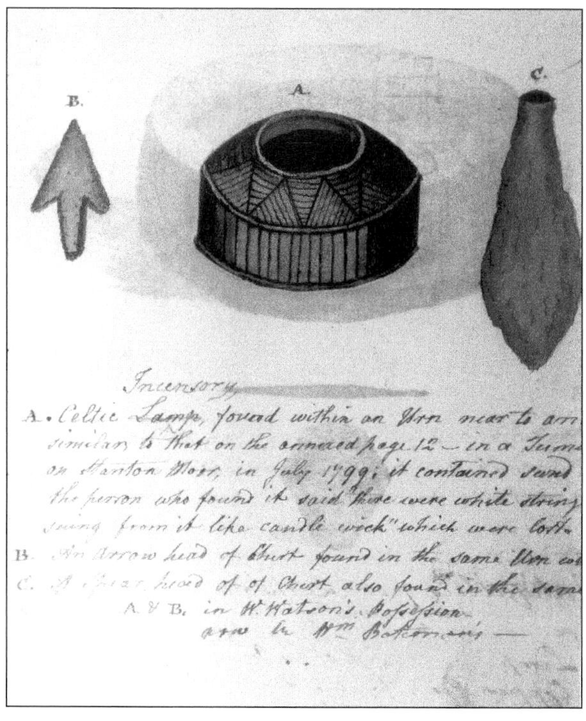

25 *Though not a barrow opener himself, White Watson (1760–1835), collected artefacts from local excavations, which he sometimes funded. This page from his notebook records finds from sites on Stanton Moor.*

Not surprisingly after this over-indulgence:

> now ensues a lengthened pause!

Isaacson recounts the visits of the curious to view the barrow-openings:

> Whilst round the aborigines
> Crowd, just as if th'industrious fleas
> Had ta'en a holiday.

If the description of the visitors as 'aborigines' seems rather harsh, it was probably justified, as the notes to Fytte IV describe the uncouth behaviour of the inhabitants of Alstonefield, Staffordshire, during the opening of the huge Steep Low cairn, echoing Faussett's remarks on the annoyances caused by 'troublesome spectators'. The work at Steep Low was 'rendered . . . impracticable by the ill-mannered conduct of the natives who thronged the low'. *The Derby Chronicle* went so far as to label them 'the most barbarous specimens of humanity between this and New Zealand'! Apparently hearing of Bateman's intention to dig at the cairn, the 'natives' had preceded him. 'In a vain search for imaginary treasure' they had dug out an intrusive Anglian burial with iron weapons and three bronze Roman coins. One of these was sandpapered into illegibility in a vain attempt to transmute the brass into gold. In *Vestiges* Bateman makes no mention of the behaviour of the spectators at Steep Low, but Isaacson wrote that they eventually forced the abandonment of the enterprise. They openly 'abstracted' bones and other relics from the cutting and crowded so close to the trench-edges that more than one of them fell in! The work was finally postponed 'till the march of civilisation shall have penetrated these benighted regions'.

In the closing fytte Isaacson relates how the cairn was restored to its former symmetry, although occasionally Bateman fell below his professed standards in this respect. The cairn on the bank at Arbor Low still shows the ravages of the opening of 1845. Bateman's final act before the infilling, following Hoare's example, was to deposit a lead tablet in the grave:

> And lest some future barrow knight
> A cutting here should make in,
> And search in vain from morn till night
> For what we've just now taken;
>
> A leaden label we enclose
> In pity to such late man,
> Where one and all may read, who choose,
> Inscribed the name, 'T. Bateman'.

Some nine of these tablets have so far been recovered from Bateman barrows; all, remarkably enough, are stamped 'T. BATEMEN', a spelling error apparently not noted at the time.

26 *Crayon sketch of Thomas Bateman (1821–61) made in 1845. A wealthy country gentleman, Bateman is famous both as a collector and explorer of some 200 cairns in the Derbyshire and Stafford Peak.*

Sadly the little volume, privately published by Bateman in August of that year at 5s a copy, was never to achieve the success it deserved, because of a quarrel between author and backer. As a result the work was never properly publicised, and Bateman seems to have sat on much of the stock. In future years, acquaintances who were presented with *gratis* copies were warm in praising its 'spirited and tasteful . . . freshness and vigour'. It was also lauded as 'an amusing, quaint and witty little work' full of 'good poetry, originality and raciness' and as 'a spirited poem with many fine touches of feeling, and not a little humour'. The poem has clear and abiding literary merit, in fact it is a minor masterpiece of English antiquarian literature. Bateman remains the only English archaeologist to have had his activities recorded in a book of narrative verse; in fact in 1870 the writer Elizabeth Meteyard published a story for children, *Dora and her Papa*, in which the main character, Walter Flaxdale, was again based on Bateman himself.

Besides *Vestiges* Bateman also wrote *Ten Years' Diggings in Celtic and Saxon Grave hills in the Counties of Derbyshire, Stafford and York* (1861). He also published a *Descriptive Catalogue* of his collection in 1855, and was preparing a further one at his death. The actual accounts of his excavations were written up shortly after they took place, in fine handwriting in manuscript notebooks. These formed the basis for his printed works. Only part of *Vestiges* concerns the diggings carried out by his father and himself, the other part concerning itself with Derbyshire antiquities of other periods. Bateman was a careful, if pedantic recorder, and the accounts of his work are clear and precise. Dates of digs are always supplied, and these show that few of the cairn openings lasted longer than a day. Sometimes more than one mound was attacked during the same day, and on one regrettable occasion between dawn and dusk four cairns at Hind Low near Buxton were dug into, rather carelessly and badly. Despite his claims to explore 'with the utmost care and preciseness', using 'the scrupulous care so necessary on these occasions', it appears that at Hind Low Bateman echoed the faults of his predecessor Hoare by employing labourers without supervision. He noted that 'the labourers (being left to themselves) were not sufficiently careful in their researches'. However, at the end of this strenuous operation, he had the hindsight to comment that 'nothing decisive could be ascertained, except a conviction of the impolicy of attempting to explore so many barrows in one day'. Generally however, Bateman was more careful than this one unfortunate occasion might suggest.

In *Vestiges* Bateman occasionally falls into the trap of misidentifying late interments. Anglian burials are more than once labelled 'Romanised Britons', although once an iron knife is regarded as 'of the kind attributed to the Saxons by the modern school of antiquaries'. These doubts are resolved in his second work, where Anglian interments are usually correctly assigned. *Vestiges* suffers most from a lack of illustrative material, the only drawings in the barrows section are of gravegoods. In his books Bateman follows Hoare's terminology with regard to pottery identification, but introduces a type unknown to the former, the 'vase' now termed a 'food-vessel'.

Diggings contains rather more illustrations than its predecessor, including sections and ground plans of certain cairns. These well executed engravings were the work of Llewellynn Jewitt, a friend of Bateman, who nevertheless received no credit for them in the preface. Roach Smith wrote in his *Retrospections*: 'it is to be regretted that Mr Bateman did not more fully avail himself of his [Jewitt's] artistic ability. I suspect that the volume

27 *An imaginative reconstruction of the burial rites at a beaker round cairn, drawn by William Bowman for Bateman's* Vestiges of the Antiquities of Derbyshire, *published in 1848.*

is in other respects indebted to the gentleman.' Jewitt, a very fine artist and a prolific writer on his own account, illustrated all the archaeological finds in the Bateman collection in a large volume, now in Sheffield Museum, called *Relics of Primaeval Life*. Here the pottery, flints, jet ornaments and other artifacts are superbly recreated in watercolours, so well executed that they have since been used to re-identify grave finds whose provenance had been lost. The manuscripts of Bateman's printed books, particularly *Diggings*, are likewise profusely illustrated with Indian ink drawings of the gravegoods and numerous plans of graves and cairns. Another large sketchbook, named *Illustrations of Antiquity*, contains blue monochrome watercolour sketches of cairns, graves and sites, mainly the work of Bateman, but with contributions by Carrington. The illustrative work and notes in the Bateman manuscript collection, and his correspondence, also preserved, present a wealth of valuable material on Bateman and his archaeological undertakings.

As far as methods were concerned, Bateman's were those of his times. His usual technique was to drive sections from some point on the cairn edge to the centre, or section the mound by dividing it into quarters. Some ground plans of Carrington's digs in Staffordshire show some rather eccentric cuttings meandering in all directions across certain mounds. The central-shaft method was apparently considered discredited by Bateman, since in his very first dig, at Bee Low, he regrets that trees growing on the sides of the mound made it 'impossible to excavate it in a proper manner', and the only tenable method of digging was 'by sinking a shaft down the centre'. Although his work on a particular mound usually lasted

28 *The excavation of Taylor's Low, Wetton, May 1845, the frontispiece for* Barrow Digging by a Barrow Knight, *Isaacson's poem describing a typical barrow-opening expedition in the spring of that year. Identifiable participants include Bateman (with pick), Isaacson (with trowel), Benjamin Thompson (with spade), Parker (to Thompson's left) and Nutt the greyhound. Next to Bateman is an interested spectator.*

only a day or part of a day, occasionally he returned, like Carrington, to mounds that he felt would repay further excavation. Bateman rarely supplies details of time expended in actual digging, but at Moot Low a 30ft cutting entailed 'six hours heavy labour'. His descriptions of cairn structures were occasionally lengthy and precise, though usually only where the construction differed from the usual kerbed stone heap. Thus a large mound on Ilam Moor was 'composed of alternate layers of earth and loose stones … these strata were clearly defined, there being no admixture of stone with the earthy layers, or of earth with stony ones'. An earth mound at Gorsey Close had its soil 'interspersed with alternate layers of moss and grass … the number of these alternations was twelve'.

Bateman's descriptions of burials and their settings were usually well and clearly written. He dealt carefully with inhumations, usually preserving the skulls and long bones. Perfect skeletons were removed and re-articulated. *Diggings* includes a descriptive list of crania exhumed by himself and his confederates.

29 *Dubbed 'the Pioneer' in Isaacson's poem, Bateman's barrow-digging friend and later brother-in-law, William Parker, is here depicted as 'A Distinguished Barrow Opener'.*

Bateman often mentioned the presence of animal bones in his cairns, sometimes with the bodies, sometimes in the mound material. Among the most singular and interesting animal bones were those of 'rats' — the remains of water-voles found in profusion in many of his sites, often in close proximity to interments. These vole bones do not occur regularly in barrows in any other area of Britain. Sometimes their positions are unspecified; at other times definite relationships were observed. At Brier Low and other sites human bones had been apparently badly gnawed by the rodents. At other cairns, such as Eldon Hill, Musden Hill and Bitchin Hill, skeletons were 'embedded' and covered in water-vole bones. Yet some cairns surprisingly yielded no rodent remains; in others certain interments were accompanied by vole bones, others were not. Bateman's evidence

30 *'A leaden label we enclose . . .' One of Bateman's lead tablets, a ritual he copied from Hoare and Stukeley. Note the spelling error common to all nine examples so far recovered.*

shows that in some cairns masses of rodent bones were available on site on the funeral day. At Musden Hill water-vole remains were blackened by smoke from a nearby cremation fire; at Blackstones Low rodent bones occurred with a cremation in a cinerary urn — all the bones were calcined. It would appear that some times the bones had been placed in the graves (perhaps they were part of the local diet) and sometimes they appear to be natural, as it is likely the burial mounds were favoured by the rodents. One other suggestion is that cairns under construction or left open for a considerable period of time could have provided places on which owls or other predatory birds disgorged or dismembered their prey. Interestingly enough, Bateman rarely found water-vole bones in Neolithic, Roman or Anglian contexts. Perhaps in the early part of the Bronze Age there was a real abundance of the rodents in Derbyshire, lasting long enough after that time to form deposits of large numbers of bones. This 'rat bone' phenomenon was also remarked on by subsequent Peak District diggers such as Jewitt, Bagshawe and Pennington. The author himself has noticed their considerable presence around skeletons in cairns excavated by him. Bateman and Carrington regarded their occurrence during digging as an almost infallible indication that inhumation burials were close by; as Isaacson put it:

Intent to find the bones of rat,
For these afford a certain trail,
Which lowe-explorers never fail.

by

A BARROW-KNIGHT.

in

Six Fyttes.

with notes

by

AN ESQUIRE.

Dignus Vindice.
Hor.

31 *The title page of Isaacson's poem, showing a cist found in a cairn on Harthill Moor, Derbyshire. All the burials were by cremation, hence the skull and long bones appear by courtesy of artistic licence!*

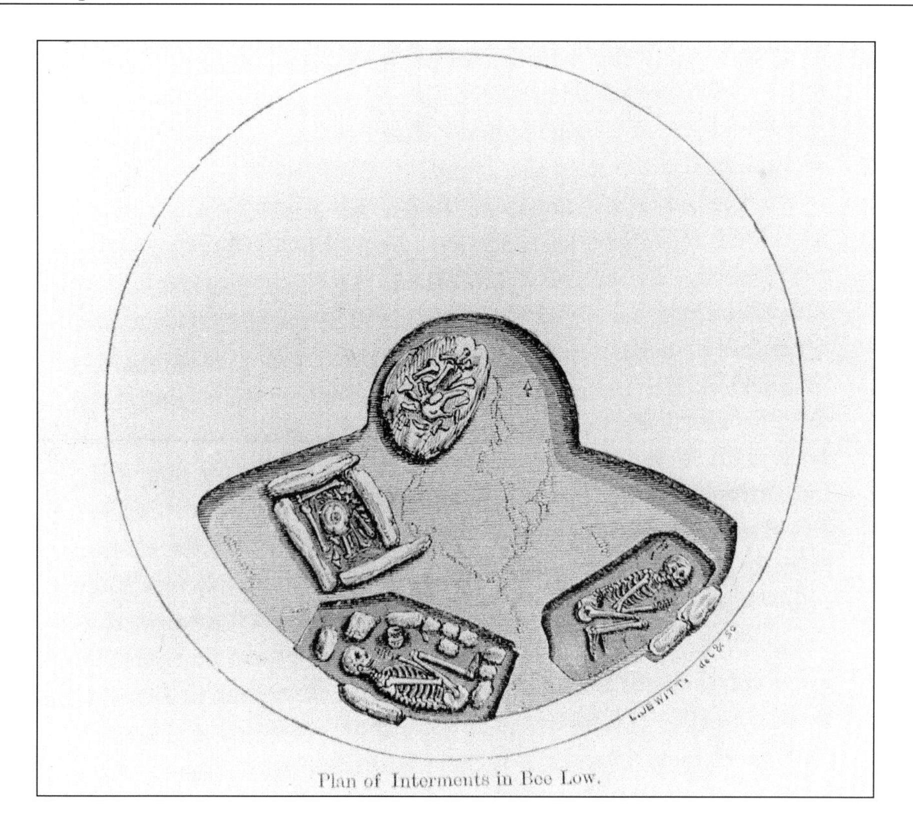

32 *Plan of the Bee Low cairn from* Ten Years' Diggings. *Bateman's woodcuts were well in advance of other barrow drawings in contemporary books, but note the large undug area, excavated by the author in 1966–8.*

The occasional humorous incident is revealed in Bateman's accounts of his labours. In 1848 his party dug into the huge Gib Hill cairn, an undertaking that lasted seven days. So large was the mound that a tunnel was driven into its side; a sketch in *Illustrations of Antiquity* shows this tunnel, supported by timbering. When no interments came to light, the supports were knocked away preparatory to filling in. The roof of the tunnel immediately collapsed, bringing down two orthostats of a large limestone cist revealed in the upper structure of the cairn. A food vessel from inside the cist also fell into the tunnel. Fortunately no one was injured in this collapse of the internal part of the mound.

Describing a skull found by his father at Kens Low, Bateman's father, William, perhaps influenced by the growing interest in phrenology, remarked, following Dr Hibbert's report, that it exhibited 'phrenological developments indicative of some of the worst passions incident to human nature'. This opinion of the unfortunate long-dead individual leads us to regret that modern anatomical reports are not so entertaining! Some of Bateman's excavations seemed highly dangerous to the diggers. Near Gotam his labourers cleared out a rock-grave sunk 9ft below the cairn surface, including 4ft into solid rock. At

33 *Bateman's excavation party attacking the huge Gib Hill cairn in 1848. The tunnel shown in the sketch later fell in, revealing a cist set high up in the mound.*

the bottom of the grave, 'by the help of a candle, part of a human skeleton was obtained from beneath an immense stone which could not be removed'. Other deep graves were at Shuttlestone, Parwich (8ft below the ground surface) and at End Low, 6ft deep in the limestone rock. On Burton Moor three skeletons were exhumed by undercutting the mound immediately below the junction of three field-walls! Bateman again relied on candle-power at Rusden Low, where a grave was found at dusk. 'Owing to the lateness of the hour at which this interment was found', he wrote, 'we were obliged to clear out the grave by candlelight.' The illumination provided by this method of lighting must, one feels, have been somewhat inadequate to say the least. While most of the excavations were planned affairs, he describes one casual dig when a stone circle, Doll Tor, was discovered during a stroll near Stanton Moor. The small party borrowed tools from the nearby farm and hacked out the centre of the site!

Samuel Carrington (1798–1870) was Bateman's lieutenant in Staffordshire. A village schoolmaster and smallholder at Wetton, he was described by Roach Smith as 'a very intelligent man; a good geologist; and an enthusiastic excavator of tumuli'. He noted penetratingly: 'Seldom are such men appreciated and I fear he was not an exception to the fate of the worthy unselfish poor'. Carrington appears to have begun working with Bateman in the spring of 1845. Some useful information on his operations appears in a large manuscript volume in his neat handwriting, once in the Bateman collection, and

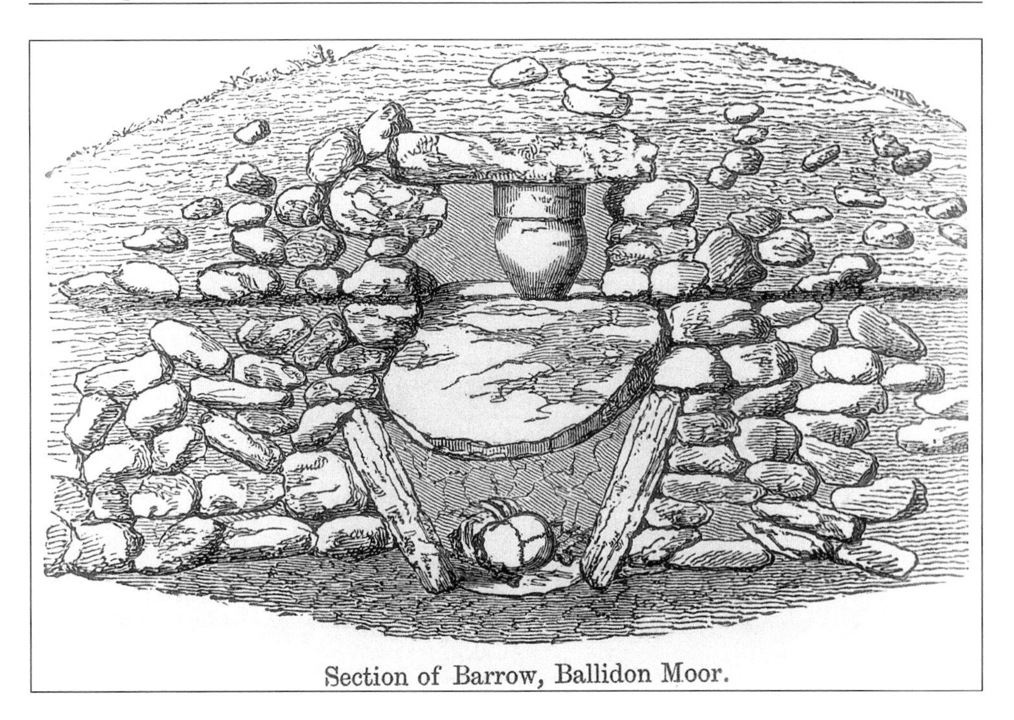

34 *A fine drawing of a cairn section in* Ten Years' Diggings, *again far superior in depiction to others of the time. It shows a primary skeleton in a cist, with a secondary urn placed on the earlier capstone.*

now in Derby Reference Library. The body of the volume is taken up by a play on barrow digging, almost certainly inspired by the work of Woolls and Isaacson. It is titled *The Barrow Diggers' Restitution of the lost Archives of Ancient Britain . . . also a Defence of the noble science of Barrow-Digging and Archaeology in general.*

The play itself, written in 1851–2, is a laboured and turgid work, but it contains some interesting observations and information. Chief characters are the First and Second Barrow Diggers. The first is obviously Bateman, and the second, likened to a lesser satellite revolving around a far greater orb, is just as certainly Carrington himself. The narrative contains some shrewd comments on digging, mainly gleaned from actual experience. In the text Carrington noted that he had dug 135 cairns between spring 1845 and autumn 1852, though this must include re-openings. Among other things he remarks on the camp-followers who come to observe the digs and who are 'disposed to laugh at them for what they call following a queer business', especially as one of his characters comments on the rewards of barrow-digging by revealing 'they find nothing . . . but bits of flint and rotten pitchers all over scratches and the potter's finger nails'. One of Carrington's truisms is worth quoting — 'No one ought to open a barrow that has not as many eyes as an Argus, and every one wide awake'.

Although Bateman only records Carrington's excavations from the beginning of 1848, between that date and 1858 the latter dug into some 100 burial mounds, mostly in

35 *Bateman's excellent private museum at his mansion, Lomberdale House. The archaeological material from his diggings was only part of his vast collection. Note the skulls and long bones in the case at the back of the room. His prehistoric assemblage was the only part to remain complete after the museum contents were sold off in 1893 and 1895. This is now in Sheffield City Museum.*

Staffordshire, not including numerous re-openings of tumuli previously explored by him. His work tailed off after 1851, probably because most of the cairns in his area had by then been rifled. The latter part of the Carrington manuscript contains letters sent by him to Bateman, describing his work on Bateman's behalf, and listing the costs incurred for labourers, and — a recurring item — for ale and beer to sustain them. Significant to relate, the cost for two men and a boy for one day was 3s3d! For one man, a 5-hour stint paid ls 'and a little beer'. Evidently Carrington paid small sums for flints found during digging, and 6d was given to some nameless individual 'for finding barrow and getting leave'. At Mare Hill he had 'three men hard at work from noon till night', as well as one 'that assists of his own will'.

Carrington also provided the original version of the oft quoted dig where the excavators found an urn, deliberately smashed it, and distributed the pieces among the diggers as mementoes. Carrington names the culprit as Thomas Mycock of Waterfall, who dug on Calton Hill, finding bones, 'besides breaking up an urn with their hacks, the fragments of which were distributed among these rustic antiquaries'. The colossal cairn at Steep Low, already mentioned by Isaacson, was dug into from time to time, but its very size foiled Carrington's attempts. At length he determined on a full-scale assault by employing two

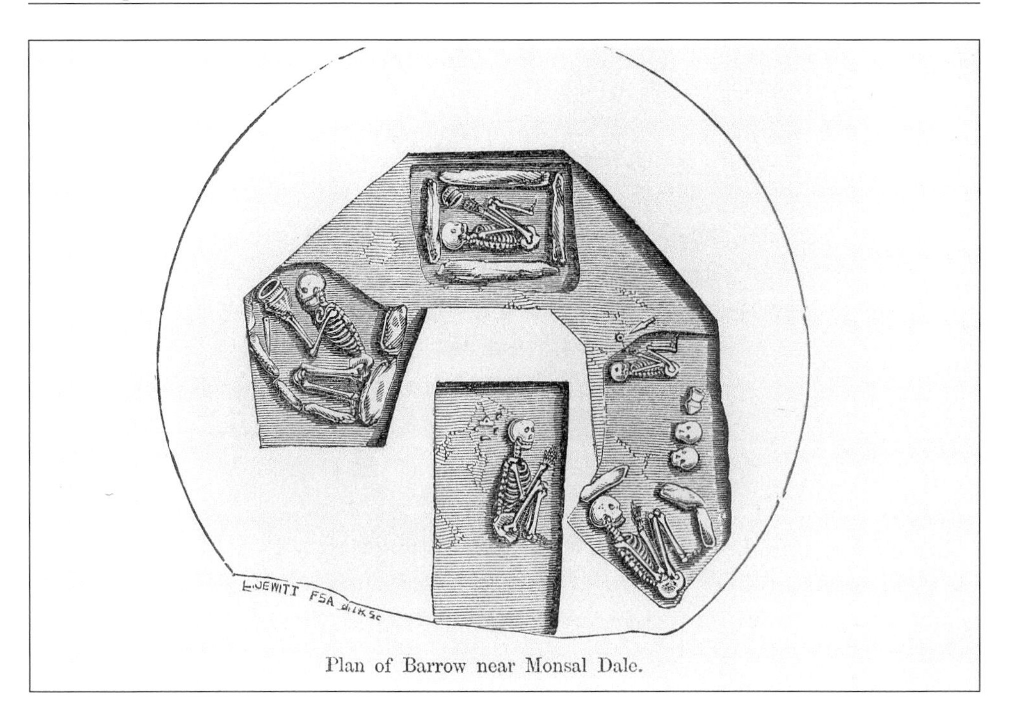

Plan of Barrow near Monsal Dale.

36 Another skilful woodcut by Lewellynn Jewitt showing one of Bateman's cairn plans, though the straight-cut sections and the perfectly preserved skeletons should be treated with some suspicion. The youthful burial in the cist at the top however was in good enough condition to be rearticulated and placed in a glass case.

men, continuously working, for 14 days. As he himself could not be there in person all the time, he arranged that 'if they met with any interment . . . they will set up a signal as I can see the barrow from the school window'! Unfortunately this prolonged operation was, like its predecessors, unfruitful, though the gallant pair opened a yard-wide cutting down to ground level to the centre of the massive tumulus. Once when opening a cairn, Carrington found an extended skeleton which seemed of recent date. Two old people in the neighbourhood informed him that the burial was that of a suicide, one Francis Brown, who had hanged himself. It appears that Brown had been wrongly suspected of taking his own life, as years later two criminals had confessed just before their execution at York, that they themselves had robbed and murdered the unfortunate man.

Carrington was always loath to leave any partly revealed burials overnight for fear of interference to them by casual curio-hunters. He mentioned helping James Ruddock on certain diggings near Pickering in 1848. The pair left a cist and the cremation it contained overnight, intending to excavate it fully the following morning. Although they were on the site by 4am they found that the cist had already been rifled. When, late one evening, Carrington found an undisturbed chamber in the Neolithic round cairn at Long Low, he sent a hastily scribbled note to Bateman, written late at night, stating that he intended 'to open it as soon as light in the morning to prevent mischief'. Carrington appears to have been a most conscientious and worthy servant. He had a deep interest in archaeology and proved a scrupulous and enthusiastic antiquary. More than once he apologised in his letters to Bateman for his lack of success in certain cairn openings, as though the fault were personally his. His deference and respect for his part-time employer come out in his description of the character of the First Barrow-digger in his play, and in his letters where more than once he describes himself as Bateman's 'sincere but unworthy servant'. He once compared himself as 'but the fly that sat on the chariot in Easop' (*sic*). Bateman dedicated his 1855 *Catalogue* to Carrington, 'as a slight acknowledgement of the assistance derived from his indefatigable zeal in the pursuit of science, by his sincere friend, Thomas Bateman'. Later articles in the *Reliquary*, and notes in Jewitt's diary show that Carrington continued to interest himself in archaeology for many years after Bateman's death.

Bateman's proxy digger in North Yorkshire was James Ruddock (1813–58). Details of how he came to be employed appear in Bateman's voluminous correspondence in Sheffield Museum. In the note in *Diggings* announcing Ruddock's death, Bateman wrote that the former 'was for many years . . . singularly imbued with an enthusiasm for Antiquarian pursuits. In his case the ruling passion (and it was no less) was strong in death'.

Ruddock was apparently a much more rough and ready digger than Carrington, and his reports were more scanty. Canon Greenwell wrote that his notes varied in quality. In one place in *Diggings*, Bateman wrote: 'were it not for the extreme accuracy of Mr Ruddock's notes', yet in another page comments on 'the vagueness of the original notes'! Although Bateman and Carrington occasionally failed to locate their own sites with precision Ruddock's own locating was casual to the point of non-existence. It was of the 'six miles north-west of Pickering' order, and has effectively prevented the re-identification of barrows dug by him unless they stood close by well-known landmarks such as Cawthorn Camps. In fact Ruddock's notes were as scanty as his locations, and on his death in 1858 his excavation records were only complete to 1854. Hence numerous barrow and casual finds including flints, pottery, stone axes and jet ornaments were passed on to Bateman with only the most vague information as to where they were found.

From *Diggings* it would seem that Ruddock dug around 100 barrows, plus the sites of others, but other sources indicate that his full score was in excess of 300! Ninety of these were on the limestone hills around Pickering. A few others were near Whitby where Ruddock lived for the last few years of his life. Whilst at Whitby he poached on the preserves of the formidable Reverend John Christopher Atkinson of Danby by digging on Eskdale Moor. Ruddock told the curious that he had permission to excavate from the guardians of the Lord of Danby Manor, then a minor. A doubting employee of the estate informed Atkinson of his suspicions. Atkinson set enquiries in motion and found out 'the entire falsehood of the statements made'. However, by this time the mounds had been rifled and the contents sent on to Bateman! Ruddock thus appears as somewhat of a dissembler. Unfortunately, besides scruples, he lacked scientific method and his scrappy notes have lessened the undoubted importance of the work he did.

Bateman's death came suddenly late in August 1861 in the 40th year of his life. He was only ill a short time (of an 'organic disease') and appeared to be on the mend when he had

37 *The imposing tomb occupied by Bateman and his wife behind the old Middleton Chapel is surrounded by decaying railings, and is surmounted by a stone replica of a Bronze Age urn.*

a relapse. At his death he had personally opened 200 tumuli; Carrington dug into a further 100. Between them they had therefore plundered 300 burial-mounds in the Derbyshire and Staffordshire Peak. Bateman's character was touched upon by Jewitt in a memorial notice in the *Reliquary*. If we siphon off the thickly spread adulation and mawkish, overdone Victorian sentiment from the account, we gather he was a man of strict principle, of a shy disposition, cold and lacking geniality to those who did not know him, but of a generous and kind disposition to his friends. He had 'a singular fondness for everything related to the past and particularly to the dead. Nothing could be more interesting to him than researches and inquiries connected with the tomb'.

He could on occasion exhibit rather petulant annoyance. At the Canterbury Congress of 1844 he was among those who visited Heppington to see Faussett's great collection of Anglo-Saxon antiquities. As the exhibition was in a small room, Roach Smith guided the visitors through in small numbers to prevent overcrowding. Dr Godfrey Faussett, grandson of Bryan Faussett, hearing that Bateman was in the party, asked to be introduced to him, so Roach Smith, wishing to give Bateman ample time to speak to the Doctor, asked him to join the final group waiting to see the exhibits. Mortally offended at being asked to wait, Bateman took himself off in a huff, although later when the reasons were explained to him, he apologised for his behaviour.

Like others of his time, Bateman found difficulty in breaking down the chronology of the burials he disinterred, though he distinguished a stone age followed by one of metal. He established to his own satisfaction the priority of the dolichocephalic (long-headed) skulls from the chambered cairns of his area, to the brachycephalic (broad-headed) skull forms from the round cairns, and probably coined the saying 'long barrow, long skull; round barrow, round skull'. He assigned the chambered cairns of the Peak 'to the most remote antiquity, when the sole material for the spear and arrow was flint'. Round cairns, with the 'short round form' of skull were correctly placed in a later era. Bateman regarded the cairn-builders as living 'centuries, perhaps tens of centuries before the lust of conquest tempted the Roman Legions across the Channel', but could go no further. They remained 'Celtic'. In *Vestiges* he attempted some inaccurate division of burials and gravegoods into periods, but said little more about these theories in his later work. Bateman was laid to rest on a hillside at Middleton behind the chapel built by his grandfather in 1827, among his beloved Derbyshire dales. It seems fitting that his mausoleum, surrounded by an iron rail, is surmounted by a stone replica of an Early Bronze Age cinerary urn.

6 Diggers or desecrators?

Barrow digging gained impetus during the 1840s, and in many areas where tumuli proliferated the barrow openers likewise increased. The years 1840–70 can justifiably be called the 'boom years', when the subject almost approached the proportions of a field sport. In 1851 Carrington wrote, 'in no age or nation have the investigations of the past from the contents of the tumuli been so arduously pursued as they have been of late in this Kingdom.' Many of these diggings were reprehensibly carried out, more often than not in a mere scrambling after relics. Few descriptions of the work were committed to paper, but one or two harrowing accounts, which must serve to represent many more, have been rescued. One, from J. Walker Ord's *History and Antiquities of Cleveland*, concerns a barrow opening on Barnaldby Moor in the 1840s.

'Earth, charcoal and stones were flung up by the workmen's spades', begins the depressing account. After a whole day's digging in this fashion, with dusk approaching and no finds made, the party:

> were about to relinquish the task in despair, when a lad, who was plying vigorously with his spade, cried out, "Dom it, here's a bit o' carved stean!" and was on the point of aiming a final *et tu Brute* blow at the precious relic, when the narrator leaped down, and arrested the fatal stroke.

Beneath the stone was an urn; despite the gathering dark it was safely extracted, and Ord 'held it aloft to the delighted assemblage' like a trophy! In a barrow on Salthouse Heath, Norfolk, dug in 1850, a certain Mr Bolding found 'a small and broken urn of sun-baked clay'. It had apparently rested somewhere near the mound surface, 'but its position was not clearly ascertained, for it was not observed until after it had been thrown out by the workmen'. In the same year, a certain Mr Greville Chesters described a novel way of dealing with a concreted mass of cremated bone found in a barrow at Roughton Mill. 'With great difficulty', he explained, 'we separated it with repeated blows of a spade!'

From the middle years of the nineteenth century many antiquaries began to view with growing concern the increasing destruction of the barrows of Britain in a plundering search for 'treasure'. John Akerman, writing in 1854, noted that in Wiltshire 'no inconsiderable number' had been dug into 'under the hands of pseudo-antiquaries'. He revealed that 'scores of our primaeval tumuli have been explored in a manner so careless, as to jeopardise the contents and often to reduce them to fragments'. In his *Celtic Tumuli of Dorset* (1866) Charles Warne had much to say on the subject, since Dorset's barrows had suffered more than those of most counties from poor excavation. In the introduction to his book he remarked that:

38 The Victorians would have titled this sketch 'The Unexpected Consequences of opening a Barrow'. Here Peter Hutchinson's would-be diggers are driven off a Devon burial mound by its infuriated inhabitants. (L. Grinsell)

> the requirements, or, in many instances, the cupidity of the age, have tolerated such an obliterating spirit that a large proportion of these our time-hallowed records have passed from amongst us; and this destructive interest has . . . especially prevailed within the past few years.

He accused past diggers of:

> desecrating these time-hallowed monuments for no better purpose than the indulgence of a craving acquisitiveness and the adornment of glass cases with ill-understood relics, to be paraded for the empty admiration of those who may descend to flatter the equally vain and ignorant collector,

echoing Bateman's earlier notice that the disappearance of barrows was, in a large part, due to 'the ill-conducted pillage of idle curiosity'.

The theme was becoming a heated topic by the mid 1860s, leading John Mortimer, who had commenced his vast operations in the East Riding of Yorkshire in 1863, to write in the *Reliquary*: 'It seems a great pity that . . . barrow diggings are not better conducted, and the examination made with far greater care and labour than what we read in the newspaper details of Yorkshire diggings'. (Was this intended as a criticism of Canon Greenwell's investigations on the Wolds, which had recently begun?) He continued:

39 *A barrow in Kent, opened under the auspices of Lord Albert Conyngham in 1844, reveals the mound under inspection by his lordship's party, with interruptions from a rainstorm.*

> I speak out as an experienced authority on such matters, and defy any antiquary to properly examine nearly twenty barrows within the month (although Mortimer himself once dug ten in thirteen days!), as was lately expressed in the columns of the leading newspapers . . . I sincerely pray these remarks may for the future prove of service, by putting a check to the speculations of the curiosity seeker, and of the individual who is actuated by that 'cursed spirit of gain' which has in late years spoiled so many of our Yorkshire tumuli.

He begged antiquaries to 'perform the work well and most scientifically, instead of hacking up a great number in an incredible short time'.

As editor of *Reliquary*, Jewitt added his own remarks on the subject, condemning the 'hasty, indiscriminate, and incomplete manner in which some of the Yorkshire tumuli have been opened', which 'called for some kind of serious rebuke from genuine antiquaries, and from those who love the science which they have espoused'. He wrote of 'wholesale destruction . . . by persons of whom better things ought to be looked for, of barrows on the Yorkshire Wolds'. Jewitt felt that 'notoriety and display, not science and genuine research, are the objects of the explorers and ransackers of the barrows.' He described the whole process as 'an archaeological battue, the object of which is to destroy the largest number of barrows in the least possible time, and to "bag" the spoils in order that the unenviable achievement may be duly chronicled in the *Times* and other journals'. He added: 'It is not the number of barrows which can be opened — "done" as the common galloping-tourist's expression is — in a "season" (genuine archaeologists know no "seasons", and no "campaigns")' but the scrupulous, careful examination of a few 'when circumstances are favourable and time can be devoted' that bestowed a lasting benefit on prehistory and prehistorians.

It would have been pleasant to report that the growing awareness of wholesale barrow-mutilation and destruction was arrested by the protests of the enlightened, but, unfortunately, bad excavation was not a prerogative solely of the nineteenth century. It is an evil that has endured well into the present century. Coupled with the careless obliteration wrought by modern agriculture, and the expansion of industry and building programmes, it has led to the eradication of a vast number of burial mounds — destruction that could ill be afforded.

7 Wiltshire

From about the time Thomas Bateman was beginning his operations in Derbyshire, barrow digging was being vigorously prosecuted in a number of other English counties. Workers of varying degrees of skill and competence were carrying out programmes of barrow research in Wiltshire, Dorset, Yorkshire and elsewhere. Since an attempt to list all the busy enthusiasts and assess and examine their work would take a vast amount of space to narrate, only the work of the more important — or notorious — will be included, beginning with the activities of some of the better-known Wiltshire antiquarians.

One of the most notorious of these was Dean John Merewether of Hereford, (1797–1850) who between 18 July and 14 August 1849, opened some 35 barrows on the Marlborough Downs. These included Silbury Hill and the West Kennett long barrow! This concentrated despoliation was afterwards written up from Merewether's notes and published posthumously in a small book called *Diary of a Dean* (1851). The publication shows that the Dean was a most enthusiastic barrow digger, who like others of his ilk, derived great pleasure from his researches. He dedicated the book 'as a legacy to my native County whose antiquities I began in early life to study'. The text shows that he had undertaken previous barrow investigations — he certainly accompanied Sir Richard Hoare on operations in the early 1800s — but no records of these appear to be available. He casually mentions visiting one barrow on the Downs, almost on the bank of Wansdyke, which he had dug some 30 years before.

During his earlier career the Dean had attracted the favourable attention of William IV, after serving as chaplain to the Duchess of Clarence, later Queen Adelaide. He became Dean of Hereford in 1832; the king appointed him a Deputy Clerk of the Closet and asked Lord Melbourne the Prime Minister to favour his future advancement. However, Merewether seems to have become increasingly bitter as episcopal vacancies occurred and he was consistently passed over. He was so soured by his experiences that when the Reverend Dickson Hampden was proposed as Bishop of Hereford in 1847, he strenuously opposed the selection, and refused to affix the seal of the Dean and Chapter to the document recording the Bishop's formal election. He wrote to the Queen, and indicated his intentions in a long letter to Lord John Russell, the Prime Minister. Russell's reply was as short and sharp as Merewether's had been long and rambling. 'Sir,' he wrote, 'I had the honour to receive your letter of the 22nd inst. in which you intimate to me your intention of violating the law.'

One of the Dean's most ambitious schemes in 1849 was the work on Silbury Hill, which was financed by the Royal Archaeological Institute who were meeting in Salisbury at the time; Merewether attended the congress and used his spare time to organise the series of diggings in connection with it. Silbury had been 'dug' in 1777 by Cornish tin-miners, working for the Duke of Northumberland and a certain Colonel Drax. They had sunk a shaft 5ft square down through the huge pile to the original ground surface, finding nothing, though Drax believed they had discovered the 'druid oak' over which he felt for some obscure reason the mound had been raised. A railway engineer called Blandford was contracted to organise Merewether's workmen who were to drive a tunnel into Silbury from the south side. Mortimer later wrote of this excavation that:

> It could hardly be expected that these two small openings would be likely to find the primary grave under Silbury Hill, than two rat holes would be likely to come upon the ashes of a mouse placed under a mound 10ft in diameter.

Since Merewether could not be present all the time (he was dodging between Salisbury and his other diggings), he arranged for the labourers digging the tunnel to cease work within 2ft of the presumed mound centre. Such accuracy was beyond them and they went 7ft further! Matters were complicated when Blandford, considering he had fulfilled his contract, ceased work, and Merewether had to take over. Little was found in the vast heap, but the Dean left an urn containing documents and a lead sheet with details of the opening. This was found by the BBC-sponsored excavators in 1969 when they were seeking, more scientifically, the answers that the Dean had been looking for over 130 years previously. Incidentally, Merewether's tunnel, barely wide enough for two people to by pass each other, was still negotiable in the early years of the twentieth century, until it was finally blocked by the Office of Works shortly after the First World War.

Merewether's book contains some sketches of inhumation burials, and some of the pottery and artefacts found, together with ground plans of certain earthworks. Little is revealed concerning his methods of opening, though the brief mention that 'the men were sent to commence operations on two mounds of large dimensions' suggests the continuing malpractice of directing unsupervised labour gangs to wreak unchecked havoc on luckless barrows.

The Dean records some of the diggings as 'laborious', due to the size of certain of the mounds. One cutting went 10ft deep, another 12. In this last opening, 'the closeness of the soil . . . and the depth we had to descend, occupied more than usually of our time, and the evening was far spent before we reached such a depth in the other barrow as to satisfy our curiosity.' These two barrows last referred to were 'distinguished by traditions which ranked them highly in the estimation of the inhabitants', as likely to prove worth investigating. Merewether took the trouble to record conversations with the local peasantry respecting local barrows. One shepherd told him how one of the shepherd boys had 'hooked up a crock' out of a small barrow on Bye Down Hill. The lad knocked the pot to pieces with his crook to see whether it contained 'treasure', and on visiting the site the Dean found the urn sherds lying around. Merewether also spoke to a man who had helped in the destruction of the Mill Barrow, a chambered long barrow near Avebury. The man recollected 'a sort of room built up wi' big sarsens put together like, as well as a mason could set them; in the room was a sight of black stuff, and it did smell nation bad'. The Dean recollected not opening a barrow inside an earthwork on the Down since it showed evidence of being dug from the apex downwards, to some depth. Thinking the

40 *Dean John Merewether (1797–1850), notorious for his large-scale excoriation of barrows on the Marlborough Downs during the 1849 Congress of the Archaeological Institute.*

hole to be the work of an antiquary, he 'did not deem it prudent to interfere with his work'. Later he had the 'mortification' to learn from a shepherd boy 'that his father had dug that 'un out for shelter'.

Rarely did Merewether record the constructional details of his barrows and chalk-cut graves were invariably 'cists'. Like others of his time he had occasion to note the presence of sightseers. The finding of a Roman coin hoard near the surface of a barrow:

> greatly excited the interest of the bystanders of the labouring class, who had on many occasions shewn a disposition to watch our proceedings, under the impression, which in all quarters possesses them — to my cost I know it, in some cases to the destruction of antiquarian treasure — that such excavations are made for the purpose of finding money.

A barrow examined in the presence of a party from the Salisbury Congress was felt by some of the workmen 'to be very promising, as it always sounded hollow when they passed over it; it did not however, fall to our lot, unfortunately, to hit upon the right place'. The last comment suggests a hasty and haphazard attempt at opening, more reminiscent of Hoare's work, which at least had the excuse of being 40 years earlier. In fact

Merewether felt that Hoare and Stukeley had attacked this barrow on some previous occasion. In connection with this, he recalled that the first barrow he ever saw opened, in 1814, was by Hoare. It produced a beaker burial — 'a beautiful early British vase'.

As a finale to the excavations, the night following work in unfavourable weather, a dramatic high Gothick thunderstorm set the seal on Merewether's Wiltshire sojourn. This event was 'much to the satisfaction . . . of the rustics, whose notions respecting the examination of Silbury and the opening of the barrows were not divested of superstitious dread'. It must have been a spectacular affair. The Dean described it as 'one of the most grand and tremendous thunderstorms I ever recollect to have witnessed'. It 'made the hills re-echo to the crashing peals, and Silbury itself, as the men asserted who were working in its centre, to tremble to its base'.

Merewether died in 1850. His work left much to be desired and its failures include the ever-recurrent one of not positively identifying clearly most of the sites he worked on. However, he was at least sufficiently committed to record his researches. The most abiding feeling about his 1849 visitation is its very immensity — the digging of 35 barrows in 28 days — plus Silbury and West Kennett, the former the largest ancient artificial mound in Europe, and the latter among the largest long barrows in Britain!

Another Wiltshire antiquarian, John Yonge Akerman, (1806–73) though not a prolific excavator, made some pertinent comments on the downland barrows in 1854, worth reprinting for his wry pessimism regarding the likelihood of their producing any worthwhile finds.

> Experience has taught me not to anticipate great things from excavations. I had learned long ago, that a rude and crumbling urn, or a simple heap of ashes and calcined bones, were the frequent result of a whole day's digging in these early sepulchral mounds, besides the possibility of our working long in one which had been explored by some previous investigator more intent in the acquisition of treasure than the procuring of antiquarian relics.

Nevertheless he was 'persuaded that such excavations were not altogether profitless'! Incidentally, the year following Akerman's 'tedious, irksome and laborious' operations, William Cunnington (1813–1906) was busy re-excavating barrows on Roundway Hill, previously dug by his more famous great uncle. Cunnington dug into seven barrows in the area, producing a somewhat idealised illustration of a beaker burial found in one mound.

The Reverend William Collings Lukis (1817–92), a scholar of European fame, was active among Wiltshire barrows at Collingbourne Ducis (Cow Down) between 1855 and 1861, and later at barrows in Yorkshire. He was of a Guernsey family whose head was Frederick Corben Lukis, opener of a number of chambered tombs on his native island and in many ways ahead of his time. Lukis *pere* realised and urged the importance of recording the find spots of casually found prehistoric artefacts such as bronzes or stone implements, and the value of sketching them — here perhaps were the germs of distribution maps plotting the occurrences of such finds. His observations on the burials found in megalithic tombs were very much in advance of their time.

41 *Silbury Hill, one of the Dean's targets in 1849. His digging party hewed a tunnel some 260ft from the south side of the monster heap to its centre.*

Lukis had noted as early as 1837 the presence of parts of bodies and accumulations of bones in the tombs of Guernsey, and felt that the burial of these part-bodies was some sort of rite. His ideas foreshadowed modern interpretations of temporary preburials of bodies at special mortuary sites. He wrote somewhat pertinently to Thomas Bateman:

> I am informed that in China . . . the body is buried temporarily, and when denuded of flesh the bones are taken up and carried to the tomb with great pomp. If such was the custom during the Stone period much of our observations will have their full explanation.

He also noted that 'the discovery of parts only of skeletons within cists ... is worthy of examination ... and perhaps too often attributed to past disturbance'. Lukis's observations show a refreshing and original slant on burial customs, and indicate a far-sighted thinker. Many of his ideas had elements of truth in them that only became evident much later in the minds of more modern archaeologists.

W.C. Lukis was a third son; other offspring also inherited the love of archaeology from their father. Frederick Dubois Lukis, younger brother of William, embarked on an army career, yet he too found time to indulge in barrow digging, in Guernsey, Brittany, Derbyshire, Anglesey and Ireland. On a brief antiquarian sojourn near Buxton in 1865, recorded in the *Reliquary*, he wrote to his father 'I indeed felt truly happy in again

42 *A lead plaque left by Merewether as a memento of his opening of Silbury. The photograph below it shows the partly blocked tunnel, still passable in 1920.*

following that pursuit which you have taught us almost from our cradle to take delight in'.

Lukis's report of work at Cow Down contains a good plan of the barrow cemetery (though no scale is shown). There are also stylised plans of some barrows and a few sections, plus sketches of the main finds. He dug 17 barrows in the group. In the *Wiltshire Archaeological Magazine* and later in the *Yorkshire Archaeological Journal* he had some harsh things to say about Hoare's operations, although having the advantage of hindsight he neglected to recall that Hoare was an enlightened pioneer, edging into an unexplored realm. Although admitting Hoare's 'praiseworthy aim', Lukis accused him of unwittingly 'doing as much as any man could to prevent archaeologists from knowing, to the full extent, what his vast researches and extensive experience should have taught him respecting Wiltshire barrows, and to mislead barrow diggers of a later day'. He deplored the loss of information relating to the construction of barrows which was not recorded by Hoare, and also:

> how many articles of antiquity of great value have been overlooked and lost through the mode in which he prosecuted his researches. If he himself had handled the spade, or been continually present with his labourers . . . we should not now have to lament the unscientific opening of innumerable barrows.

Lukis recalled that had he followed Hoare's methods in digging the Collingbourne group:

'the largest barrow would have been an enigma, and I should have wondered why so vast a cenotaph had been raised'. Lukis's strictures on Hoare's central-shaft opening technique are interesting, since a famous contemporary of his, Thurnam, was still using the method in his own Wiltshire diggings.

While recognising the value of the early excavations of Hoare and Cunnington, Lukis complains that:

> in many cases we have difficulty in ascertaining the material of their construction; the site of the interment within the barrow is frequently only implied, instead of being accurately noted . . . we are led to the conclusion that the chief, if not sole object, in the investigation was the possession of the articles which had been deposited with the dead.

Lukis returned to this theme, rather unfairly, in an article on some barrow diggings in the *Yorkshire Archaeological Journal* for 1871.

Lukis's usual *modus operandi* was to drive a trench into a selected barrow, usually from the south side, e.g. 'we dug a wide trench from the south point to the centre, and in some cases beyond the centre, and next we carried trenches east and west from the south side, at a few feet from the base of the mound'. These latter trenches curved round to follow the shape of the barrow. The trench system outlined above revealed the primary burial if eccentrically placed, and 'brought to light a series of interments in positions where they have not been commonly observed in Wiltshire'. Even so, his diagrammatic plans, if accurate, show that large areas of some larger barrows he dug still remained untouched.

Lukis's father had written to Bateman in August 1855, giving details of his son's activities at Cow Down. He revealed:

> He is in the midst of Sir Richard C. Hoare's scene of labours and having free leave to explore over the estates around him, he has commenced his diggings recently . . . he has explored eight barrows which must have escaped the Baron's vigilance . . . His work is chiefly devoted to the surrounding low barrows, near to camps and Stations. Many of these can only be discerned by the eye of the practical digger & he leaves those elevated mounds to future examinations. The usual position of the skeleton found, is that of lying on one side bent up at the legs — with one vase near the head — singular enough that many of these subjects are not 12 inches below the grass of the plain — and yet preserved in nearly perfect state.

Lukis was a careful observer. He noted that some of the barrows in the Cow Down group had been enlarged to accommodate subsequent burials; he usually described the materials of the mounds but did not always give details of their size. An enumeration of one burial deposit will serve to show his orderly method and concise description. It refers to a primary interment found in a 'cist' deep inside one barrow. This chalk-cut grave was 3ft 10in long, 15in wide and 1ft deep. It was almost 9ft from the apex of the mound.

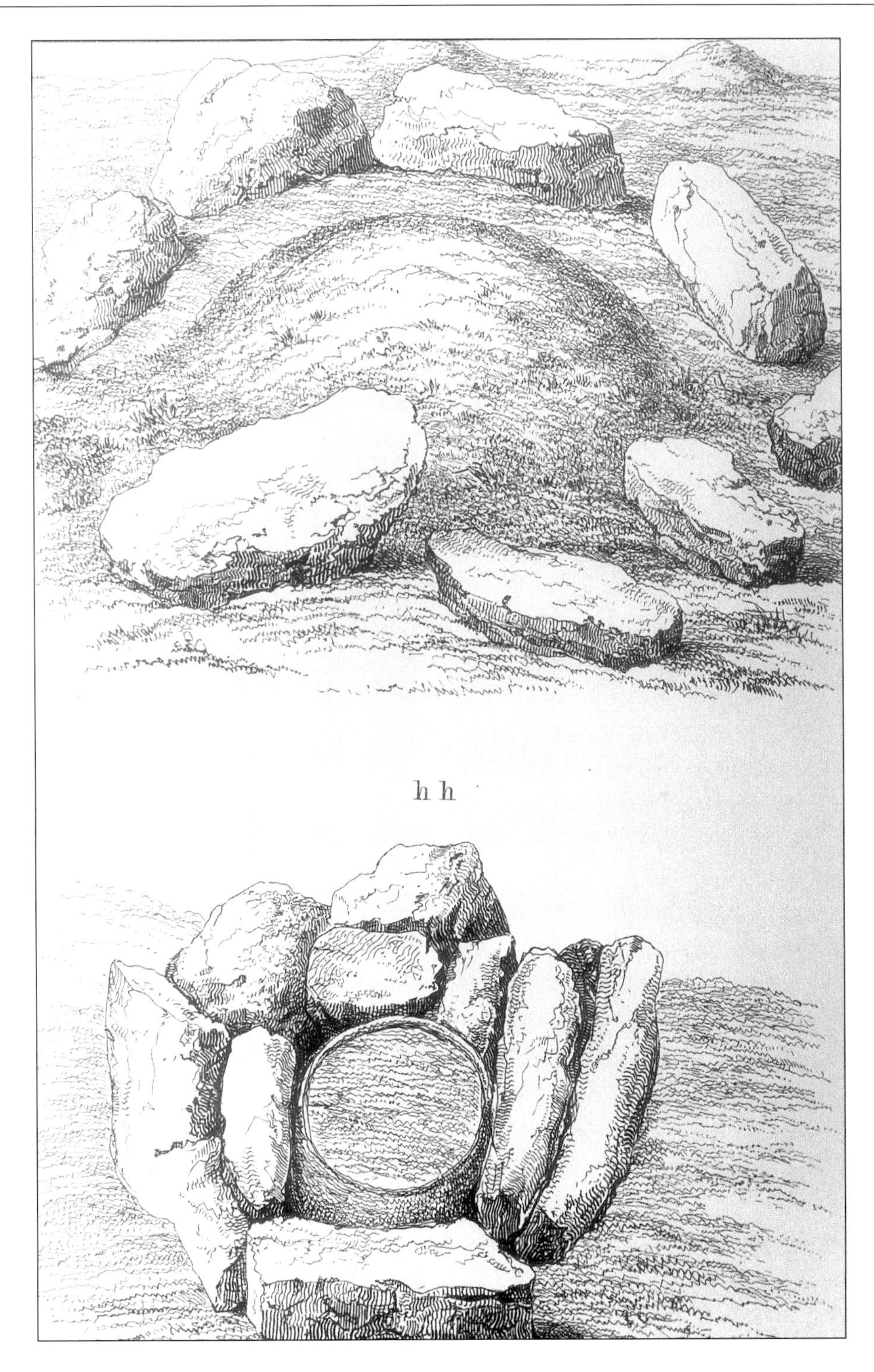

43 *Drawings from Merewether's published article on his barrow blitz of 1849, showing a barrow surrounded by a stone kerb, and a cist containing a collared urn cremation.*

44 *A much-idealised representation of a beaker burial found by William Cunnington on Roundway Hill in 1855. The skeleton reposes peacefully, wearing a satisfied smile. Often such deposits are damaged by the weight of the superincumbent earth or stones and are rarely found in such a perfect state.*

> The grave was cylindrical (he wrote) and had been lined with a plaster of powdered chalk about one and a half inch in thickness. The plaster had received the impression of the bark of a tree, and indicated that the bones of the deceased had been placed in a hollow trunk which was deposited in the grave whilst the plaster was still moist … it was found that the coffin was only partially beneath the surface level, and that it had been covered over with a similar coating of powdered chalk which, when it dried, retained an arched form over the grave after the wood had decayed. With the bones, which were calcined and those of a young person, was a horn hammer or mace head about four inches long and one and a half inch wide.

A few disquieting undertones still echo the spirit of Hoare, whom Lukis so strongly condemned. Of his barrow no. 9, he wrote that it 'was imperfectly examined by us', although 'it was our intention to explore it again on some future occasion'. One barrow in the cemetery was 12ft high. Lukis began work on it in 1856. His force started on the south side, 'but the labour was so great that the work was discontinued at the end of two days, after making little progress'. Work was resumed on this mound in 1861 with two acquaintances and two labourers. In accordance with the growing practice of seeking specialist reports on human bones, Lukis adds a footnote on a skull from the barrow, examined by John Thurnam. The barrow cemetery produced numbers of satellite urn burials (40 came from one barrow, though tree planting had damaged many of them). Lukis felt that many of the Wiltshire barrows were of large dimensions since they had been enlarged to admit these subsequent interments. He rejected the slave-sacrifice theory, as he felt the groups of cremation deposits represented family or tribal burial places.

As well as opening barrows at Collingbourne, Lukis also dug at several long barrows in Wessex. Later in the 1860s he was busy excavating barrows around the Thornborough henge monuments in Yorkshire, and was also digging up Saxon interments with Greenwell. He could not closely — or even loosely — assess the period of the round barrows he dug, 'because no one can do so with any degree of certainty', he wrote. 'Attempts of this kind have been too common and been too often based on insufficient data.' The best he could do was to give 'reasons for thinking that they belong to a pre-Roman period'. Further than that he could not go. Lukis drew a number of illustrations for Greenwell's *British Barrows*. Later still in the century he was working with William Borlase in Cornwall while researching for his *Rude Stone Monuments of Cornwall*, published in 1885.

Dr John Thurnam (1810–73) has gained fame more as an interpreter and synthesiser of barrows and their contents than as an investigator of them, though his diggings were numerous. He is justly remembered for his great monograph 'On Ancient British Barrows, especially those of Wiltshire and the adjoining counties'. Part one on long barrows appeared in *Archaeologia* in 1868, part two on round barrows following in 1871. These two papers formed the basis of all subsequent barrow study since they assessed all the information gleaned from every previous published excavation, and analysed the mound-types and the relics they contained under a series of headings. Thurnam's true importance lies in the mass of important facts he gleaned from his vast and penetrating study of tumuli. As far as his own personal excavations go, it has been said that he 'was indefatigable in exploring ancient British barrows', although, strangely for one whose analysis of barrows was so acute and progressive, his actual techniques were in many respects a retrogression on those in contemporary use elsewhere. For this reason Thurnam's real fame rests in his valuable repositories of basic information on long and round barrows, which, interpreted with perception and scholarship, are still of great value today.

During his lifetime Thurnam gained notice in several spheres of activity — as a doctor, an archaeologist, a craniologist and as medical superintendent of the Wiltshire County Asylum at Devizes, a post he held from 1851, the year of his marriage, until his death. Born near York, of a Quaker family, he was privately educated and became a member of the Royal College of Surgeons in 1834. In 1843 he became a Licenciate of the Royal College of Physicians, and a Fellow in 1859. He graduated MD at Aberdeen University in 1843. His first post appears to have been that of resident medical officer at the Westminster Hospital, which he held from 1834 to 1838. He then became medical superintendent of the Friends' Retreat in York. According to Mortimer he also held the post of curator of York Museum at the same time. In 1849 he was selected as medical superintendent at the Wiltshire County Asylum, then being built in Devizes.

In earlier life Thurnam gained some reputation as an authority on heart diseases and for his statistical studies of insanity. In Wiltshire he became an expert on craniology; he co-operated with Joseph Barnard Davis (1801–81) in the publication of *Crania Britannica*, a study of British prehistoric, Roman and Saxon skulls. He himself gathered a large collection of skulls, now in the Duckworth Museum, Cambridge.

His first archaeological investigations were on the barrow groups of the east Yorkshire Wolds, around Driffield, where he directed operations for the York Literary and Philosophical Society. The openings were hasty and uncritical, William Bowman remarking 'that pack of asses Thurnam and co. intended to go to Driffield on Monday night and commence early on Tuesday morning, finish the barrow there by noon, fly over to the Danes' Graves, open four or five of them and return to York by the last train' — a horrifying glimpse of an all-too typical mid-nineteenth century barrow expedition!

Thurnam began more thorough and systematic barrow digging in 1853. Details of his work appear in several journals, including the *Wiltshire Archaeological Magazine*, the *Proceedings of the Society of Antiquaries*, *Archaeologia* and elsewhere. He excavated earthern and chambered long barrows as well as opening a large number of round barrows, and his operations can perhaps best be described by separate reference to the three above types of burial mound. Thurnam's main preoccupation was 'bone hunting' and many of his barrow openings were concerned with the recovery of skeletal material; some of his diggings had the sole aim of relocating burials recorded but reinterred by Hoare and Cunnington. Few details of mound construction are given, apart from cursory mentions of the 'chiefly of chalk rubble', 'stratum of black earth' type.

Earthern long barrows were monuments which especially interested Thurnam, and to which he gave much attention. Between 1855 and 1867 he dug at no less than 22 of the Wiltshire ones. Some, like Bowls Barrow, he reopened to locate the burials left by Cunnington. Of those he worked on, some nine openings were, in his opinion, successful. Not all were fully reported on. His excavation methods regarding long barrows are only cursorily mentioned. One at Wilsford was heavily assaulted; in October 1866 Thurnam wrote that 'altogether sixteen holes have been sunk into this barrow without meeting the primary interment, the hope of which must be abandoned'. The long barrow at Winterbourne Stoke crossroads underwent four distinct excavations before the presumed primary burial — a crouched skeleton — was found 55ft from the east end at sunset one summer evening. Thurnam mentions a 'large excavation' at the east end of the Tilshead Old Ditch barrow, and at Bratton Castle in August 1866 his working party 'made two large openings at the extreme east end'. Incidentally, at Winterbourne Stoke a round 'cist' or hole was found near the back of the skull of the supposed primary burial. This hole was 'scooped out of the chalk rock'. It was 18in wide and 18in deep. Two similar oval 'cists' were found 2ft to the north. Thurnam regarded them as 'ritual' pits for deposits of food and drink for the dead or 'for the blood of human victims, whose mangled remains appear often to have been buried with the body of the chief in this class of tumuli'. Modern interpretations would suggest that the holes could be the post-holes of a collapsed mortuary structure covering the burial.

As one might expect, his descriptions of the burial deposits found in this class of monument are very precise. At Tilshead East Ditch barrow he found eight skeletons 'in a space of less than four feet in diameter and about eighteen inches in depth'. Of these he said:

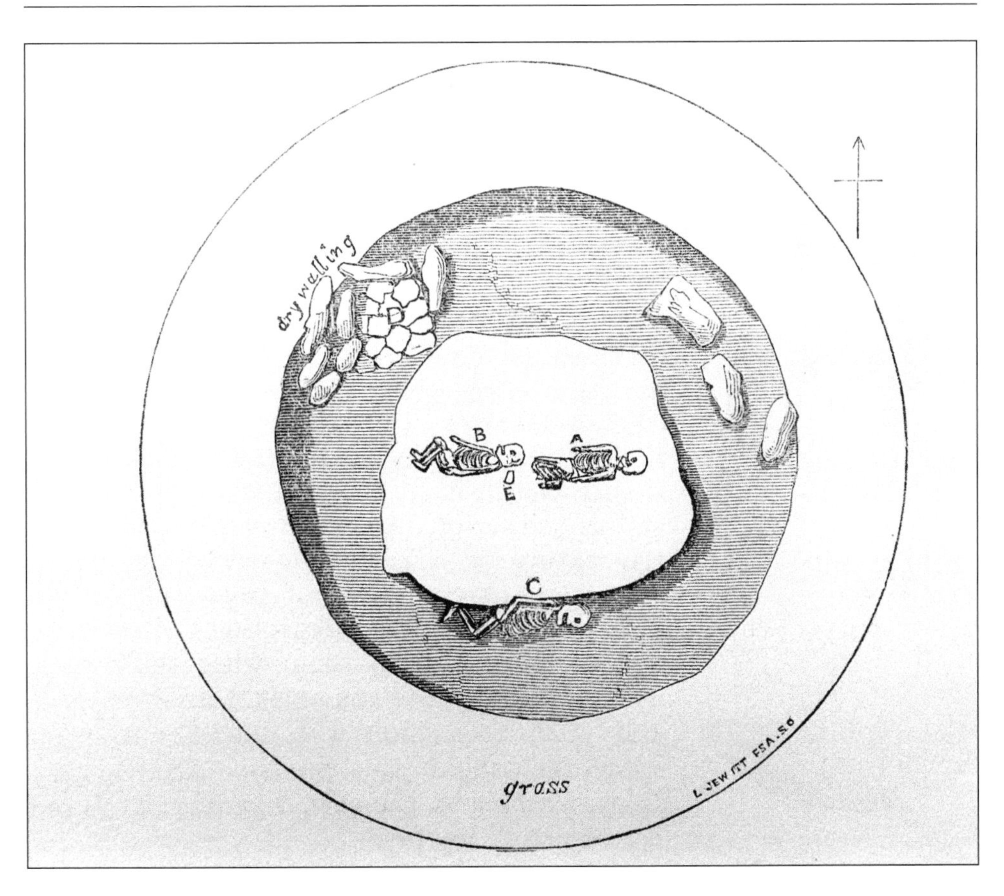

45 *While recuperating at Buxton Captain Francis Dubois Lukis found time to open the cairn here shown in plan in 1865, details of which he submitted to the* Reliquary.

> so much were they mingled and so closely packed, that it was scarcely possible to regard this as the original place of burial; and it is almost certain that they had experienced a prior interment, and had been removed to the spot where they were found after the decay of the soft parts and the separation of the bones ...

This introduced the theory that long-barrow burials were stored in some other locality before their final interment. At Norton Bavant 'there was great commingling of osseous remains; and it was noticed that many of the bones of the limbs were absent, judging as to their proper number from that of the skulls'. A Windmill Hill pot was found among the mass of bones. Thurnam's careful checking of the inhumations led to his noting this lack of limb bones. It was apparently the first time that any observer had realised that some long-barrow skeletons were incomplete, a deficiency now believed in part to suggest the abstraction of certain long bones from the tombs for ritual or magical purposes, hence their presence in the ditches of certain causewayed camps in southern England.

46 *John Thurnam (1810–73), doctor, craniologist and barrow digger, whose fame rests mainly on his syntheses of British burial mounds and his publication of* Crania Britannica. *(Roundway Hospital, Devizes)*

Thurnam was concerned, almost to the point of obsession, with the 'cleft skull-human sacrifice theory', with regard to the earthern long barrows. In five of these mounds, and in the previously dug Bowls Barrow, he found 'broken' skulls, the owners of which he felt had been sacrificed at the death of a chief (he expressed the hope that he could show the long barrows to be 'the tombs of chieftains'). He remarked, 'I hence conclude that the skeletons with cleft skulls are those of human victims immolated on the occasion of the burial of a chief'. However, there are convincing reasons to account for the cleft skulls found by Thurnam. Significantly this phenomenon only relates to disarticulated burials. Damage to the skulls could have occurred during disinterment or collection before reburial; alternatively the collapse of internal wooden mortuary buildings could have led to breakages; or they could have suffered unwitting damage during excavation. There is little conclusive evidence to support Thurnam's oft-proclaimed theory of male suttee on the Wiltshire Downs.

Quite possibly Thurnam's diggings were not extensive enough to uncover the primary burials in some of the long barrows he opened. A number of these openings appear as 'not successful' in the results published in his table in *Archaeologia*. At other times, on encountering a single bone-stack, he may have felt that the whole primary interment had been found. Yet the four 'stacks' uncovered by Ashbee at Fussell's Lodge suggest that perhaps complete burial deposits were not always obtained. Indeed Thurnam was once deluded by the filling and blocking at the West Kennett chambered long barrow into thinking the vast mound contained only one, terminal, chamber, thus completely missing one pair of transepts. The final count of measurable skulls dug out of the earthern long barrows by Thurnam was 27. He also encountered secondary burials, which he observed were 'not unfrequently met with in the upper strata, or near the summits of long barrows'. Also mentioned were occasional ox bones, sometimes in association with the burial deposits. The bones most frequently met with were 'those of the skull and feet'. Thurnam was involved in the opening of a number of chambered long barrows, some 10 of which he dug in Wiltshire and Gloucestershire. His interest in chambered barrows dated from 1849 when he read an unpublished memorandum of an opening of Hetty Pegler's Tump, Uley, Gloucestershire, preserved together with two skulls at Guy's Hospital Museum. He decided to re-excavate this transepted gallery grave with the object of drawing the ground plan, and obtaining plans and sketches of the chambers. The barrow was eventually examined in 1854.

In 1855 work was carried out at the Lanhill and Lugbury chambered long barrows in Wiltshire. He followed these in 1859 with the opening of a long barrow he had long eyed with interest — the famous West Kennett long barrow, a notable field monument mentioned by Aubrey and sketched by Stukeley. The excavations were limited by the refusal of the tenant to allow any surface stones to be shifted. Three large visible capstones suggested the presence of a chamber (the west one). This was attacked from two directions, one via the passage, 15ft of which was dug out, the other from the opposite side, 'where a party of men entered it . . . having successfully tunnelled under the large eastern cap-stone'. One of the covering stones, 3 tons in weight, crashed into the chamber during the digging, and had to be extricated. Misled by the ancient filling and the fact that the north-west and south-west lateral chambers were partly closed by blocking stones,

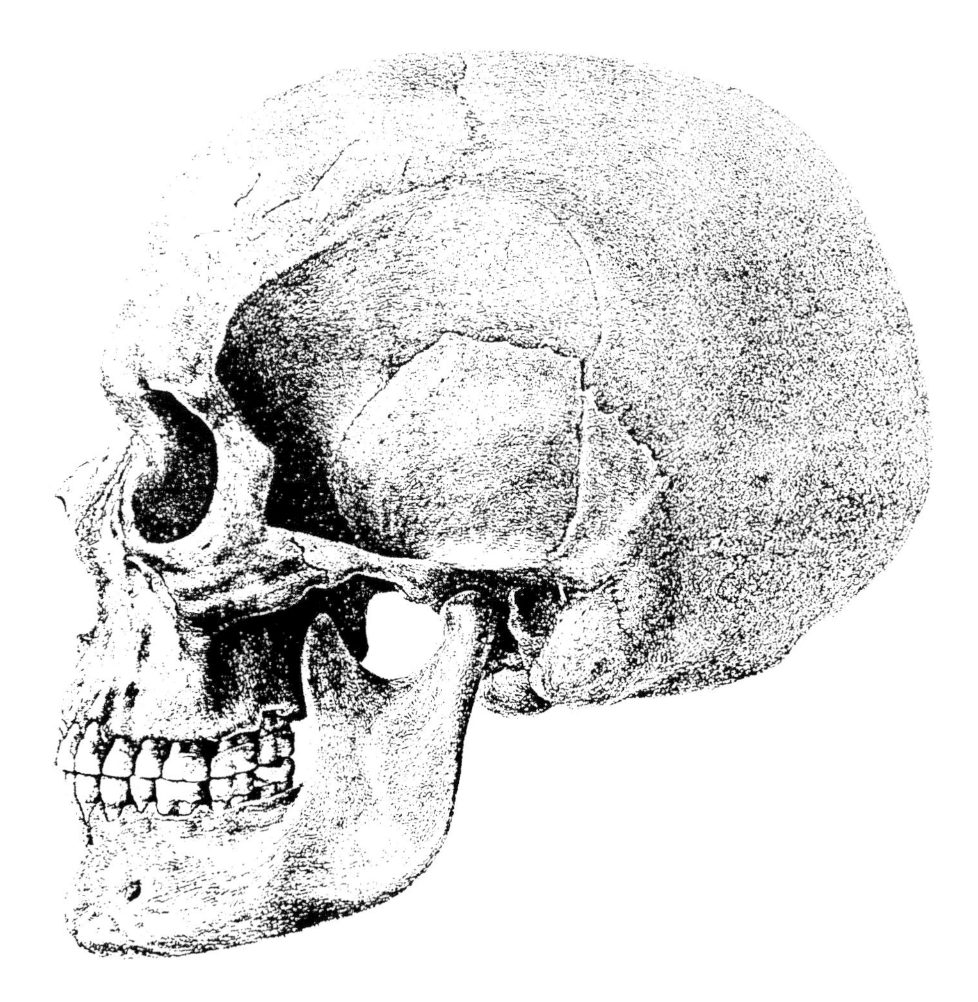

47 *Splendid lithograph of a skull from* Crania, *which Thurnam co-wrote with another craniologist, Dr J. B. Davis.*

Thurnam concluded that the west chamber was the only one in the barrow. He therefore missed the north-west and south-west transepts; the ones on the north-east and south-east were beyond the limits of his excavation. He commented on, as an unusual feature, the chamber and passage filling, which consisted of 'chalk rubble'. In the west chamber, at a depth of 5ft, was a layer 3 to 9in in thickness of a 'blackish, sooty and greasy-looking matter, mixed with rubble'. Thurnam recorded six burials from the west chamber; one had its skull fractured, allegedly before death, and another had been interred 'apparently in a sitting position'. The published 'reconstruction' of the barrow is highly misleading, as is another woodcut purporting to represent the north end of the east facade, but showing little relationship to the structures found by Piggott in 1955.

In 1860 Thurnam dug at Adam's Grave, close by Knap Hill, although its chambers had previously been rifled and only traces of skeletons were found. In 1862 he was digging in Gloucestershire with the Cotteswold Field Club. During their field excursions he assisted in explorations at Nympsfield, Bown Hill, Rodmarton and Belas Knap. He discussed the differences between chamber types and noted the false portals or blind entrances, as at Rodmarton. He remained unsure of the purpose of these structures; he felt they 'formed a monument rather than part of tomb properly so called', or 'a place where certain funeral rites were performed'.

Thurnam commented on the external structure of two chambered long barrows, after digging at their bases. He found three or four courses of dry-walling between peristaliths — the 'post and panel work' often found revetting this class of monument. Certain broken skulls found in the chambers of some chambered long barrows which he investigated led him to return again to the sacrifice theory to explain their 'cleft' nature. The Gloucestershire chambered barrows proved prolific in interments: Thurnam records a total of 70 burials from them, 15 from Hetty Pegler's Tump, 12 from Nympsfield, 13 from Rodmarton and 30 from Belas Knap.

Between 1853 and 1868, according to his records, Thurnam investigated some 61 round barrows. The last 19 he dug are not closely located and again not all fully recorded in print; next to nothing was revealed concerning their contents. All the barrows were in Wiltshire. Six of them were disc barrows in a small cemetery south of Beckhampton; again this type of barrow especially interested Thurnam, but only two of this group produced interments — cremations with miniature cups, one with a bronze awl.

Several of his round-barrow digs were into mounds previously worked on by Hoare and Cunnington; here, his interest was in recovering skeletons left by the earlier pair. One of these barrows was on Overton Hill, close by the destroyed Sanctuary. Hoare had written that the skeleton was one of the most perfect interments he had ever met with — he had 'uncovered every bone' and was 'enabled to leave it unmoved and even undisturbed'. In a barrow below Morgan's Hill Thurnam found a George III penny and a lead square stamped 'Opened 1804. W.C.'

A small, low barrow on Pound Down was proved to be the one opened in 1814 by Hoare, in the presence of Skinner and Merewether, occasioning the former's lengthy poem on the subject. Thurnam's labourers found a brass disc inscribed 'Opened by R.C.H.' Thurnam found burials in a number of barrows pronounced sterile by Hoare and Cunnington, though in 1868 Hoare's 'Monarch of the Plain', north-west of the Cursus group, proved as unproductive to him as it had done to his predecessors. Three very small mounds on Overton Hill previously attacked by Hoare, produced little, though excavations in 1962 revealed them to be circular, timber-ringed Roman tombs.

Like Bateman, Thurnam often gave the measurements of long bones, and occasionally figures of skulls. Sometimes barrow measurements were noted, but few details of mound materials were felt worthy of notice. Urns in some barrows were still mis-labelled 'sun-dried pottery'. One urn had a deep crack, with a neatly bored hole on each side, 'evidently made for the insertion of thongs or cords, by which the urn might be held together and the further extension of the cracks prevented'.

Thurnam's theories on the dating of the Wiltshire round barrows (and those on Oakley

Down, Dorset) are of interest. He felt them to be 'probably Belgic'. Beakers in general, he believed, 'could be supposed' to belong 'to a late period'. Elsewhere he wrote that beakers were 'such as are usually met with in the most modern circular or British tumuli'. In Wiltshire he decided that two separate tribes held sway, one in the northern part, the other holding the south. 'That occupying the North Wiltshire Downs', he wrote, 'appearing to consist of the Dobuni of Ptolemy, who clustered around their aboriginal fane at Avebury'. In south Wiltshire Thurnam thought that the Belgae were in control. 'These last', he continued, 'brought with them from the Continent a more advanced civilisation; probably erected Stonehenge; and doubtless maintained a more intimate traffic with Gaul than did their northern neighbours.' Another reason (to Thurnam) why the south Wiltshire tribes were more advanced than those of the north lay in the fact that their barrows were more elaborately formed, with bell and disc types in some quantity, 'whilst in North Wiltshire these are of much more rare occurrence'.

Disappointingly, this author of the learned barrow syntheses in *Archaelogia* still adhered to the central-shaft method of opening round barrows. 'Our plan', he wrote, 'has been to dig a hole, ten or twelve feet square, in the centre of the mound; and to sink a shaft from the top to the bottom, until the undisturbed chalk rock is reached, and the original interment disclosed.' To Thurnam this method preserved the external form of the barrow, though at the expense of any understanding of a mound's stratification and the high probability of missing subsequent burials. Indeed he criticised contemporary diggers in neighbouring Dorset for their insistence in following 'the much more costly and tedious method of cutting a trench through the entire mound,' as this defaced the form and shape of the barrow and, 'except in rare cases, such an extensive section cannot be requisite for the full disclosure of the contents of the tumulus'. He rightly castigated modern barrow openers who failed to restore the mounds they dug, instancing the blundering operations at the famous 'Culliford Tree' barrow in Dorset, part-dug and left open in 1858. He wrote:

> A wide trench had been dug through it on one side, from the summit and the rubble which had been thrown out had not been replaced . . . Another subject of regret was the fact that though, as we were told by the neighbouring rustics, human remains, with pottery and certain other relics, were found in the barrow, no authentic account of the exploration had, so far as we could learn, been put to print.

Speaking of his digging operations, Thurnam reminisced on 'pleasant days passed in active exercise on the breezy downs, where if, like the eastern monarch in the apologue, we have found no basilisk, we, like him, have found healthful recreation suited to our taste, the results of which, are not we think, entirely without value and interest' On a personal level Thurnam appears to have been rather stuffy, self-centred, stubborn and long-winded, though doubtless redeeming qualities were also present! When he left York for Devizes, Thomas Brushfield wrote rather unkindly that he had 'departed to join his relatives at the Wilts County Asylum'. Yet later the same correspondent could state, after Thurnam's wedding, that 'if marriage improves me as much as it has done him, I shall

48 *Dr Joseph Barnard Davis (1801–81), friend of Bateman, and Thurnam's coadjutor in the pioneering study of ancient British crania. His home in Staffordshire was so packed with specimens that the locals called it the 'Skullery'.*

have just cause to be thankful'. Brushfield could also note after one conversation with the Doctor that the latter 'used some of the longest polysyllables the English language has ever been tortured with. I expect he cannot have been taught John Bunyan's plain Anglo-Saxon.'

Relations with Davis, his co-author on the *Crania*, were at times a little stiff. Davis once commented on his coadjutor's eccentricities and 'the distance of his personal manners which those of us who are aware of their own peculiarities would be the first to excuse'. Yet he could also write:

> his is a peculiar mind. He appears to see nothing but himself in the present, and nothing but himself in the future. I am persuaded it is not a failure with him, but a sort of instinct. I am frequently obliged to oppose an unrelenting firmness, when compliance would be much more gratifying to me.

Like other men of note, Thurnam had his personal oddities and foibles, but these detract little from his reputation or the enduring nature of his pathfinding studies.

Thurnam's great study of tumuli in *Archaeologia* contains much useful information on various collections of barrow relics by contemporary excavators. He saw the many urns from the Deverel Barrow, supposedly 'safely deposited and carefully preserved', in the Museum of the Bristol Institute. It was to be regretted, he wrote, 'that they are falling to pieces and in danger of being quite lost'. Thurnam apparently travelled through the length and breadth of England examining collections and he mentions pottery and other grave goods amassed by many well-known diggers of the time.

In retrospect, it is impossible to escape the conclusion that, however highly we place Thurnam as an interpreter of barrows and their contents, as an actual excavator his methods were a retrogression on those in contemporary use elsewhere.

8 Dorset

William Stukeley, writing in the eighteenth century, felt that Dorset 'for sight of barrows' was 'not to be equalled in the world'. Yet it has also been truthfully said, in 1959 in *Dorset Barrows*, that 'in no county in southern England are the records of excavation of barrows more chaotic, through bad excavation, than Dorset'. The county has, in the past, suffered a desecration of its barrows commensurate, in relation to its size, with Yorkshire. Many burial mounds have been rifled idly and no records kept; others have been destroyed through the process of bringing former moorland and heath under cultivation. Warne remarked more than once on the sad despoliation of the Dorset tumuli, 'not a note having been recorded'. He blamed most of the pillage on 'the morbid appetite of idle acquisitiveness at the expense of science', considering that 'well may every true antiquary deplore the circumstance of a nation's earliest monuments becoming the prey of such wanton aggression'.

Two of the early nineteenth-century Dorset excavators have already been touched upon in this history — Miles and his operations on the Deverel Barrow, and Woolls and his excavation at Shapwick. However, one of the earliest Dorset diggers to record his work was Dr John Milner, who in 1790 opened some 17 barrows near Lulworth. His party seems to have camped near the burial mounds they were working on as he mentions 'pitching tents'. His work was prosecuted with the usual carelessness natural for the time. One barrow, Hanbury Toot, yielded little, but the local peasants eyed the working party speculatively and when the diggers had departed they descended in a body on the mound in the search for riches. Unfortunately for them they found only 'a heap of ashes'. In another barrow a skeleton was found which was conjectured to have been 6ft 6in tall, but 'the account of the people, however, employed in digging, had magnified it to be of the size of seven or eight feet' — a circumstance often repeated in the annals of eighteenth-century archaeology.

A most imaginative and unstable Dorset digger was John Fitzgerald Pennie (1782–1848), who opened certain barrows near Lulworth in the 1820s and 1830s. His writings show a vivid imagination and dramatic prose style well-fitted to his former, and unsuccessful, career as an actor. At East Lulworth a barrow 'in the dark brown wilds of the adjacent heath' revealed 'combustion and inhumation without urns, the ashes of the dead appearing to have been mixed up with the blood of some victim, and moulded into the shape of a globe, then laid in a small cist'. On another occasion, finding an urn in a chalk-cut grave, he recalled his feelings 'on opening the gloomy chamber of death. Who could behold the once sacred tomb of other days . . . without mingled emotions of veneration, awe and melancholy?' Pennie's fertile brain conjured up the funeral rites at the barrow, with 'officiating Druids', the 'sacrifice of slaves', and 'bloody lustrations' in the best

Gothick traditions. With a decision that modern archaeologists must envy, he fixed the status of the interment — 'This I do not hesitate to pronounce was the tomb of a Chief Druid'. Perhaps the most entertaining tale of a Dorset barrow interment came from Winterbourne Monckton in the 1830s where a mound produced four skeletons, one of which was reported to have had preserved the 'undigested contents of the stomach, containing the seeds of the wild raspberry'. These had apparently been passed on to Dr Lindley, curator of the Horticultural Society's gardens at Chiswick. He reported planting these, and they allegedly grew!

Other barrow openers active in Dorset in the early Victorian era included William Shipp and Henry Durden who, whilst officially responsible for digging some 18 barrows between 1840–60, did much more according to Thurnam, since Durden's collection, poorly catalogued, contained some 40 urns. The notes they wrote, like their digging, left something to be desired, Warne commenting they were 'somewhat brief'. The pair were very much of the 'acquisitive' school of archaeology; working on barrows near Wareham, they bemoaned the fact that they had 'laboured hard for nearly five hours hoping that something might be ultimately brought to light which would reward our toil and research'. Again, delving in a tumulus on Bulford Down, they 'commenced by sinking a shaft in the centre of the mound'. This was 'an undertaking of the utmost difficulty . . . occupying some six or seven hours'. Much of the time was spent shifting the flint cairn that so often covered burials in Dorset barrows. Eventually 'great was our mortification at finding that the result of much labour afforded nothing more than some ashes and charred wood, with a human tibia'!

Some of the conclusions reached by the pair regarding the burials they found enter the realms of pure fantasy. Finding two skeletons in a mound close to a hillfort, they conjectured with no convincing proof that the men had died 'worthy defenders' of their homes, 'their lives sacrificed in repelling some aggression made on their community'. On Houghton Down they encountered a barrow some 5ft high, composed of large blocks of flint. 'Six men were employed for four successive days [under supervision?] in removing the stones and other material.' Nothing was found, and the barrow was declared an enigma, though Warne drily remarked; 'a little more perseverance and the enigma would have been solved'.

Another barrow on Roke Down, mentioned by Shipp and Wake Smart (who himself dug a few Dorset barrows) contained a deep, chalk cut grave. This grave was in the process of being cleared out when they were 'reluctantly compelled by the infalling of night to desist, intending to renew the research the following day; in this we were unfortunately disappointed, and had no subsequent opportunity of completing our investigation'. Presumably the mound was left open by these incredibly casual investigators. The grave was finally excavated by a Mr Solly who found a cremation with three bronze daggers, one grooved with five rivets and a bone handle. Unfortunately, these priceless weapons were later destroyed by a fire that gutted Mr Solly's house

John Sydenham was another energetic digger of Dorset tumuli. Between 1839 and 1843 he opened some 25, but some of the work was done in association with Warne. Warne mentions only some 11 or 12 barrows dug by Sydenham in the county. In 1842 the Reverend J.J. Smith opened some eight barrows at Bincombe, some of them by trenching to the centre from their eastern sides. His manuscript, formerly with the Cambridge Antiquarian Society, has apparently been lost. Thurnam and Davis later wrote in their *Crania Britannica*, 'Regret must be expressed at the imperfect manner in which the whole of the excavations were conducted and their results recorded'.

Another enthusiastic investigator of tumuli was the Reverend John Henry Austen who dug 29 burial mounds in the county between 1841 and 1871. For his time, he appears a relatively careful excavator, whose accounts contain worthwhile information on such points as barrow sizes, the composition of mound structures and comments on burials. His invariable opening method was a trench, cut lengthwise, usually from the east side of the barrow. In 1845 he opened the Badbury Barrow, two-thirds of which had been previously carted away. He carefully recorded the construction of the tumulus, which had an envelope of chalk, inside which was a massive circular 'wall', enclosing an area of some 30ft in diameter. The wall was built of sandstones, and Austen conjectured that these had been brought from Lytchett, five miles away across the River Stour. The wall was firmly built and its interstices tightly packed with flints. Burials by inhumation and cremation were found in the area bounded by the wall. Shortly after the completion of Austen's work, Durden visited the site. He found on the surface at the barrow centre the now famous stone decorated with carvings of axes and daggers.

Austen also opened the Afflington Barrow commencing with a trench 'six paces broad, which was intended to have been cut completely through'. The mound was built of 'clay-like earth', so compacted and hard, 'as to require the constant application of the pick-axe'. The barrow contained a series of intrusive skeletons, perhaps Romano-British. Two of these skeletons, 'evidently those of a man and woman', were so positioned that 'the head of each leant towards the other, so that the foreheads touched so intimately that the blade of a knife could not have passed between them'. On Merley Heath one of five skulls in a barrow 'bore on it the mark of great violence, there being a fracture of the crown, as well as a transverse indenture, such as would be caused by a blow from a celt'. In a barrow on Creech Hill Austen came upon the fragment of a trepanned skull. It was lying by a complete cranium and consisted of the 'frontal section of the central orbit of the skull of a child; it appeared precisely as if it had been sawn off, and resembled a shallow basin. We could find no further portion of this skull.' He often gave measurements of the long bones of the skeletons he found and, as noted, fully described these inhumations. He correctly assigned interments which occurred in a number of his barrows, realising that one mound had 'reference to two races of people; the one the native Briton, the other his conqueror the Saxon'. Warne was not convinced about the correct identification of the latter, but from Austen's description it appears a reasonable assumption.

Austen mentions the use of labourers on some of the barrows. On Ballard Down he employed six workers who 'began simultaneously on the east and west sides, cutting a nine feet wide trench completely through'. His reports suggest a committed enthusiast who sought to explain the era of the interments he found in reasonable terms. He emerges as something more than a mere dilettante and collector, a species all too frequent on the broad acres of Dorset in the mid-nineteenth century.

Charles Hall amassed a collection of relics from Dorset barrows, and assisted in a number of openings, particularly with Warne, who describes him as 'a most enthusiastic

49 *Charles Warne (1802–87), barrow digger and collector of information relating to earlier and contemporary Dorset antiquaries.*

antiquary'. His worst fault was that he was 'unfortunately, not given to taking notes'. Warne commented that 'had he paid the same careful attention in recording the particulars of his researches, as he bestowed on the preservation of such objects as he obtained, we might now have been in possession of facts most useful to the antiquary'. In short Hall stands as a clear example of Warne's much criticised disciples of 'craving acquisitiveness'.

Charles Warne (1802–87) was himself one of the most important figures of nineteenth-century Dorset archaeology. Born in the county, he became an intimate friend of Roach Smith, with whom he toured France in 1853 and 1854, and who described him as 'a regular barrow man'. In later life he lived in London, then at Ewell near Epsom and finally at Brighton. He began researching into the burial mounds of Dorset in 1839 and did most of his work between that date and 1862. The results of his extensive diggings were recorded in his *Celtic Tumuli of Dorset* (1866). This book is divided into three sections, entitled 'My own personal researches', 'Communications from personal friends', and 'Tumuli opened at various periods'. The last two parts describe barrows opened by his acquaintances and predecessors. Roach Smith, perhaps blinkered by his great friendship for Warne, describes the work as 'for the true antiquary . . . the best that has been written'. According to Roach Smith, Warne's later volume, *Ancient Dorset*, 'places Mr Warne in the foremost rank of antiquaries'. From the modern standpoint, however, his work was typical of its time, particularly in its failure to pinpoint accurately the barrows he dug, for future researchers. His vagueness is reflected in such casual locations as 'Pokeswell Down on the Ridgeway', 'Third milestone from Dorchester on the Bridport Road', and even 'Blandford Down, near the Telegraph'!

In the preface to his book, Warne remarks that the questions 'who were the Ancient Britons, and by what races were the tumuli of Dorset and Britain raised' were problems 'which although supposed to be long since set at rest, are even now far from being satisfactorily determined'. His own conclusions merely restate that 'the obscurity which now on every side surrounds all things connected with the era in which they lived, is almost, if not wholly impenetrable'.

Warne's excavation methods, even if not always strictly adhered to, were based on close observation and recording. He writes:

> It becomes the duty of every practical investigator not merely to cultivate and exercise habits of minute observation, but likewise most sedulously and accurately to record every peculiarity that is presented . . . in the course of his researches.

Of the Dorset barrows, he remarks that they involve 'much useless labour without, in the opinion of those whose sole desire seems to be the furnishing of their cabinets, producing any commensurate reward'.

Warne's investigation reports generally include descriptions of the composition and structure of the mounds and the excavation methods employed, usually involving 'driving a passage from the eastern side towards the centre'. Some smaller mounds were often sectioned. Between 1839 and 1862 he excavated some 46 round barrows, often with the help of friends and hired workmen. One of the major difficulties experienced by Warne in his work was the extraction and preservation of urns found in the chalk-cut 'cists'. In one mound on Osmington Charity Down a fine urn was uncovered. It was:

> perfect in form and ornamentation … the deposit seemed but of yesterday … Congratulations were exchanged and opinions given as to the safest method of removing this interesting discovery from its last resting place, when we had the intense mortification of seeing it gradually crumble to pieces from its sudden exposure to atmospheric influence, without being in any way able to arrest the progress of destruction.

On other occasions urns proved difficult to rescue — one from a barrow on Pokeswell Down fell apart despite the 'greatest care' in its removal. In fact, a number of urns were found in the barrow, but few were capable of preservation as they had been penetrated and broken by fibrous roots. Another urn, found in a barrow near the 'third milestone from Dorchester', also crumbled on exposure to air.

Although most of Warne's investigations took at least a day to complete — and sometimes much longer — on one regrettable occasion he dug into seven barrows in one day, 8 September 1848. The barrows were on Gussage Down. One had been previously dug by a labourer accompanying Warne's party. He had found a large urn which was 'destroyed in attempting its removal, the fragments still remaining scattered about'. Warne mentions seeing another carelessly dug barrow on Steepleton Down. He wrote that this tumulus 'had been opened or rather scraped out by a shepherd boy; portions of an urn, the results of his profitless labour, were scattered about'.

Some of the barrows dug by Warne were of large size and proved hard work to open. One on Came Down, later removed 'to promote the fertilisation of a crop of turnips', contained some 2,000 cart-loads of soil. Often 'much time and an immensity of labour' or 'a considerable amount of time and labour were expended' in these openings. A barrow on Lords Down, Dewlish, 'required such fixedness of purpose in the determination to proceed with the investigation, that none but antiquaries who were very deeply interested in such researches would be prepared to encounter'. A rather poor drawing of a section of this barrow appears in Warne's book. Elsewhere he writes that opening one barrow was 'a work of considerable labour, with for a long time nothing to occupy our attention'. Another at Bincombe 'was equally laborious and its result was unproductive'.

Some barrows dug by Warne had been previously damaged by ploughing. One on Upway Down had been almost swept away. Among the debris he 'discovered the bottoms of nearly twenty urns'. Indeed, poor excavation and agricultural destruction together appear to have created havoc on the barrows of the county. Warne's conclusions regarding certain interments travelled deep into the realms of unsupported speculation. A series of urn cremations deposited at apparently short intervals in a barrow were regarded as 'the relics of some wild warriors, who had fallen in two successive passages at arms with neighbouring tribes; for we cannot imagine that any ordinary family sepulchre would have closed at one and the same time over so many of its members'. Twenty urns were unearthed at this barrow opening. They most likely represented the burials of a family or tribal group, placed in the mound at intervals, or, if Warne's idea of a near-contemporary mass of interments

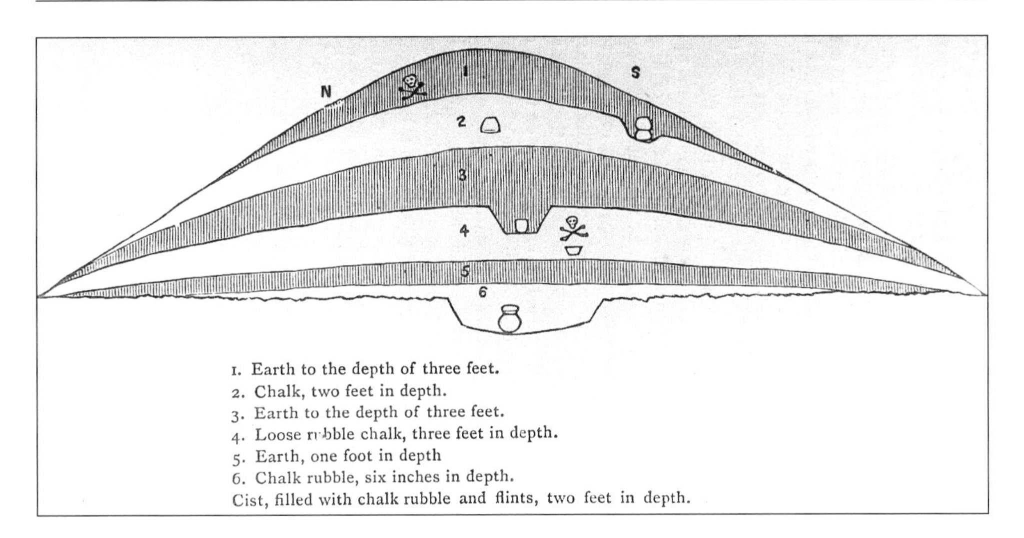

50 Section of a barrow on Lord's Down, Dewlish, in Warne's Celtic Tumuli of Dorset *(1866). Compare this rather inadequate effort with the section drawn in Bateman's earlier Ten Years' Diggings (Plate 34).*

was in fact correct, they suggest the depredations of some epidemic sweeping the area. Most probably his interpretation of the time-span of the interments was faulty.

Like other contemporary diggers, Warne invariably referred to chalk-cut graves as 'cists'. He reserved the term 'kistvaen' to describe a stone-built tomb. He laconically remarks finding one of these latter receptacles when passing through the deep cutting of Ridgeway Hill on his way to Weymouth. On his left he saw a stone projecting from the turf near the summit of the hill. It proved to be the end stone of a kistvaen containing a skeleton, 'which probably yet remains as I left and saw it long afterwards'.

One of the most pointless examples of vandalistic destruction which Warne reports in his book was that wrought by some labourers on a flat cremation cemetery at Rimbury. A report reached Warne that 40 urns had been found in a field during agricultural operations. Of these only two had survived the attentions of the 'rustics', who smashed many of the 'crocks' in the vain hope of finding riches in them. Warne writes that the men themselves, on being questioned, admitted that annoyed at not finding treasure, they wreaked their vengeance on the luckless vessels 'by placing them as marks at which to exercise their skill in throwing stones'. Warne records that on his arrival at the site 'the surface of the adjacent ground was thickly strewn with the debris of the urns — relics of the labourers' wrath'.

Warne's work at Rimbury disclosed a number of urns that had escaped the wanton destruction of the workmen. Again, it seems that the material of which the pots had been made was deficient, 'as 'altho' the greatest care was taken in their removal, and that by well practised hands, it was absolutely impossible to prevent their disintegrating'. Only a few urns survived from this important cemetery whose pillaging was a dire commentary on the avarice of the local workmen and their primitive lack of care over the remains of these remote inhabitants of Dorset. This sad episode has affinities with one at King's Newton, Derbyshire, where labourers digging a cutting for the Midland Railway in 1866 came upon an Anglian urn cemetery. Finding that the urns did not contain the hoped-for treasure, the workmen amused themselves by smashing the pots. Llewellynn Jewitt recorded in the *Reliquary* that one unenlightened individual 'sent his pick axe through seven at a stroke'.

Warne emerges as the most capable of the earlier Dorsetshire archaeologists. He was much more than a mere 'pot-hunter', and justifiably censures the poor 'excavation' work carried out in the county in the nineteenth century. Typical of this pointless ransacking was the opening of Culliford Hundred Barrow, already mentioned by Thurnam. It was investigated in 1858 on the orders of a local magnate. No one noted down any facts attendant on the excavation, 'which was but partially effected'. It was this spirit of destruction without profitable gain that so bedevilled the county's barrows at a time when better things might have been expected.

In common with his contemporaries Warne failed to break down the mystery surrounding the period of the barrows he dug. He could not assign to the many burials, mostly cremations, he unearthed any close era. To him they remained hidden in an 'obscurity' that was almost 'impenetrable'. As a narrative of barrow opening in his county, Warne's book is an important record. However, he has little to add to the theories of his fellow mid-nineteenth-century barrow investigators as far as advancing knowledge of the era and the builders of the Dorset tumuli.

Edward Cunnington of Weymouth (1825–1916), a great nephew of William Cunnington the elder, was busy excavating Dorset barrows in the last three decades of the nineteenth century. In his old age he wrote up the accounts of his diggings in a manuscript notebook presented to the Dorset County Museum by his son and daughters in 1915. It records in spidery, shaky handwriting details of Dorset hillforts, Iron Age settlements, Roman sites, and has a long chapter titled 'Particulars of Barrows'. Cunnington had hoped 'to publish the results' of his 'excavations and discoveries', but for some reason he never did, consequently his notebook, and a series of watercolour sketches of barrow plans, sections and gravegoods provide the only remaining details of his work. From his writings and other sources it seems that he dug some 53 barrows, mainly around Dorchester and Weymouth. The late Major Harris, long domiciled in Derbyshire, but born in Dorset, remembered Cunnington in the late 1890s, then an old man. Harris's father and Cunnington were friends, and Harris himself, as a young boy, often served in the capacity of the latter's bag-carrier during diggings in his last years. Harris remembered well the austere old man, dressed in a dark frock coat green with age and a pancake hat, looking much like a parson, although Cunnington was evidently no friend of the clergy — a reverend volunteer working on one of Cunnington's barrows apparently smashed an urn with an inadvertent blow from a pick-axe. Thus the whole fraternity earned Cunnington's undying antagonism!

Edward Cunnington achieved fame in the pages of Thomas Hardy's writings as the model for his antiquary in *A Tryst at an Ancient Earthwork*, a short story in the volume *A Changed Man and other Tales*. Hardy described him as:

> a man about sixty, small in figure, with grey old-fashioned whiskers cut to the shape of a pair of crumb-brushes. He is entirely in black broadcloth — or

51 *Edward Cunnington (1825–1916) strikes a Napoleonic pose in this studio portrait of the Dorset antiquary. Cunnington opened some 53 barrows in the county during the latter part of the nineteenth century. (Dorset Natural History and Archaeological Society at the Dorset County Museum. Photograph Ref. P.14.611 via Elizabeth Cunnington)*

> rather, at present, black and brown, for he is bespattered with mud from the heels to the crown of his low hat. He has no consciousness of this — no sense of anything but his purpose, his ardour for which causes his eyes to shine like those of a lynx, and gives his motions all the elasticity of an athlete's.

The story presents a picture of illicit digging by lamplight at the Roman temple on Maiden Castle, ending with the purloining of a statue of Minerva, now in Dorchester Museum. This supposed theft annoyed his great niece Elizabeth Cunnington, who wrote in 1975 'but Edward would not have kept the Roman statuette, as Hardy makes the antiquary do'!

In Chapter One of his manuscript Cunnington discusses the structure of Dorset barrows. Usually, he wrote, they produced 'a mere handful of calcined bones . . . covered by loose stones near to form a cairn, and then surmounted again by rough clods of loose sandy peat'. Cunnington described from time to time his excavation methods on certain mounds. Thus one was 'opened by cutting into the centre from the south side'. The famous Clandon Barrow had a section driven right through it. From Cunnington's drawing it seems that this section, 6ft wide at the top, opened out to about 10ft at its deepest, thus dangerously undercutting the excavation. Perhaps for this reason the opening did not penetrate to the primary burial. A long barrow at Bradford Peverell was opened 'throughout its length, by a trench varying from 2 to 4ft in breadth', with 'also a transverse cut across the broadest part, and variations wherever a change of the soil invited further inspection'. A bell barrow on Came Down 'was opened on the north side by a cutting which was enlarged considerably as it approached the centre, and dug down to the hard chalk throughout'. In terms of time most investigations seem to have taken one or two days to complete. On a few occasions more time was needed. The Clandon Barrow took six days to cut through and other large ones must have taken a similar amount of time judging by their sizes and the eventual depth of the cuttings. Cunnington usually gave the dimensions of the barrows he opened, including the heights from the old ground surface at their centres. Some trenches went very deep; one opened in a barrow on Whitfield Farm went down to 17ft before the primary skeleton was reached. A trench into his Ridgeway 7 barrow went to the same depth and one cut into Ridgeway 8 descended to 11ft. The next barrow — Ridgeway 9 — had a trench 'cut 4ft broad, 11ft deep, and 14ft long'. Cunnington often mentioned the mound materials revealed by his trenches. His deep kistvaens or large stone cists were sometimes constructed of Portland stone. One capstone of megalithic proportions, from a barrow at Fordington Field, was 'evidently an outlier from the Portland beds at three miles distance'. Its weathered upper surface led Cunnington to think it had lain long exposed on the ground surface before it had been dragged to the barrow to serve as a capstone. The skeleton in this cist had been provided with six superb flint arrowheads with square-cut barbs. The Herrington Barrow had a capping of gravel, then a cairn of stones below, so typical of Early Bronze Age Dorset tumuli. A cairn structure in a barrow on Whitfield Farm 'was irregularly made, in some places appearing like a double arch with earth between, and extending about 12ft'. The Clandon Barrow, 68ft across and over 18ft high, was 'composed entirely of layers — put in with some regularity, of the sand clay and gravel'. Cunnington felt that the earliest round barrows he opened were those built up of local surface material found nearby. One

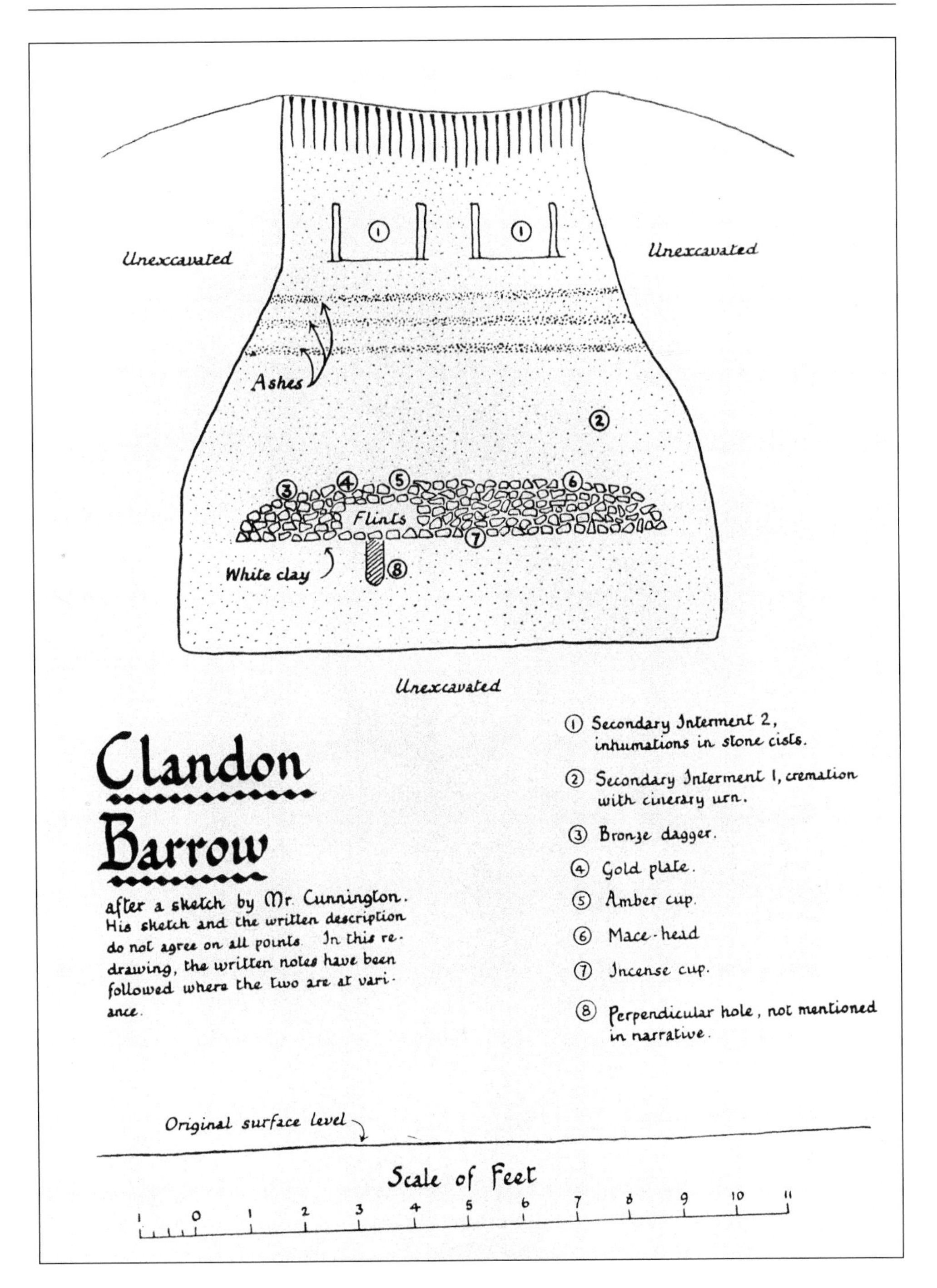

52 *Section of the Clandon Barrow, opened by Cunnington in 1882, redrawn by C.D. Drew from the former's original sketch. Note that the cutting never reached the old ground surface, rather fortunately considering the dangerous undercutting shown in the illustration. (Proceedings of the Dorset Natural History and Archaeological Society)*

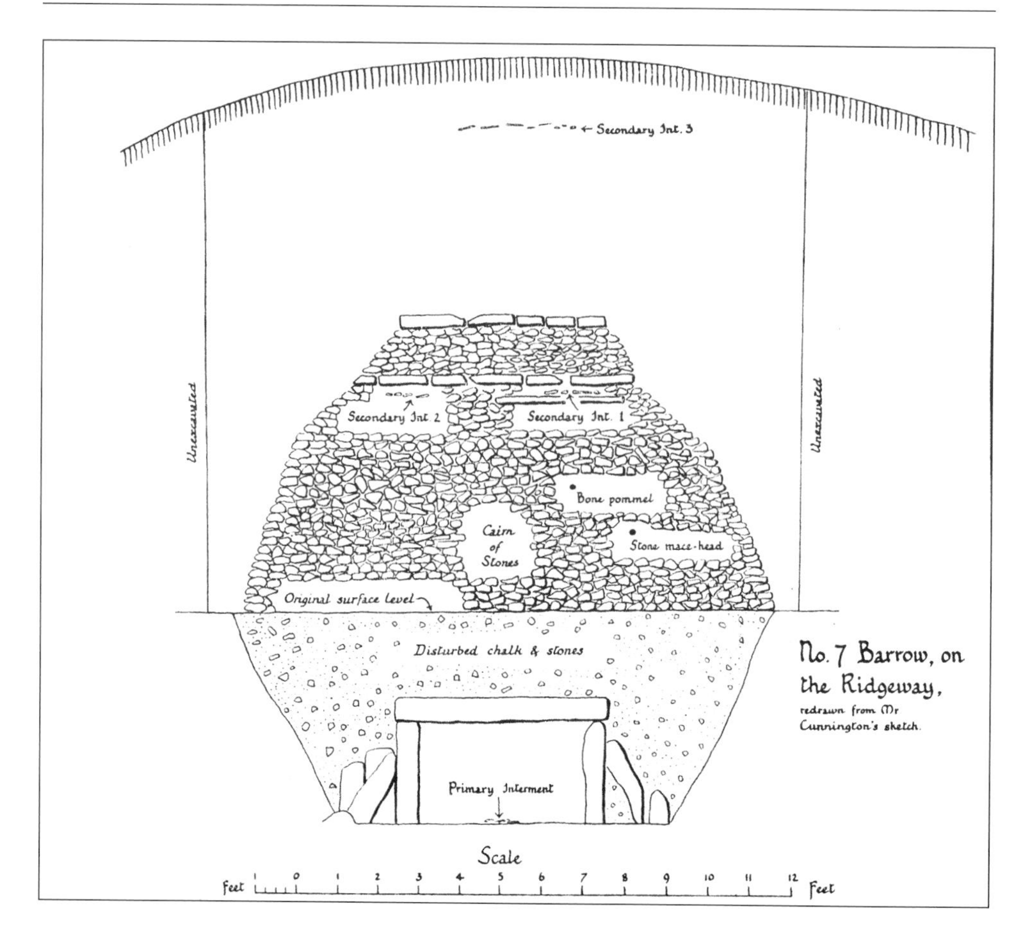

53 *Section of Ridgeway 7, opened in 1885 by Cunnington, again redrawn by Drew from the original. The amount of work involved in building — let alone uncovering — the structures, must have been immense. The section is some 18ft deep to the base of the cist. (Proceedings of the Dorset Natural History and Archaeological Society)*

of these 'was almost entirely composed of the adjacent top surface, the means and tools for utilising the harder chalk being probably lacking'. Another similar one was made 'almost entirely of the surrounding surface soil'. A barrow on Puddleton Heath proved to cover, 4ft below the surface, 'an enormous heap of large rough stones collected from the immediate neighbourhood'. Alternately, his Ridgeway 12 was 'formed of the tertiary sands and gravels which occur at this point'.

Cunnington often provided useful details of the skeletons found during his excavations and often solicited expert help in their examination. Thurnam examined some skulls from a barrow found under the Roman vallum at the south-east corner of Dorchester, pronouncing them 'undoubtedly ancient British'. Professor Rolleston (also Greenwell's cranial expert), examined other bones, although on one occasion Cunnington noted with regret, 'unfortunately I never had particulars of the bones from

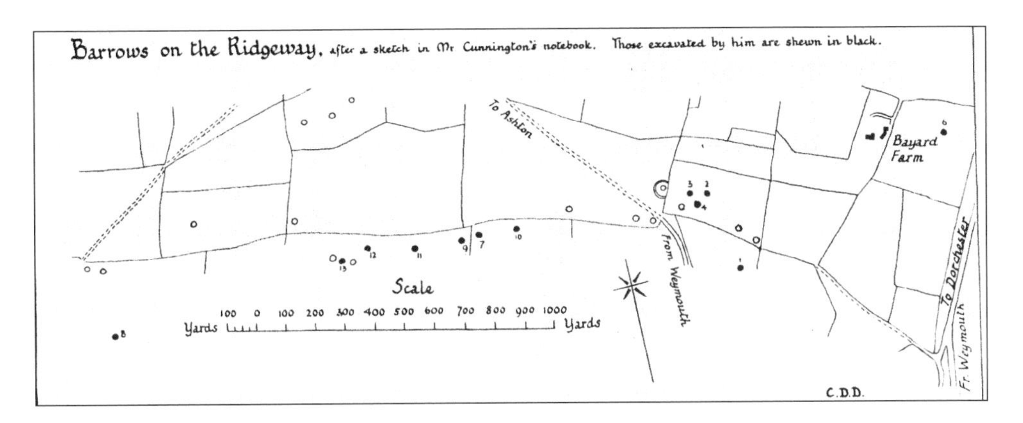

54 *Sketch map showing the Ridgeway barrows, and the positions of the 12 dug by Cunnington, from his original plan. (Proceedings of the Dorset Natural History and Archaeological Society)*

the late Prof. Rawlinson' (sic). Rolleston wrote specialist reports on other inhumations. One from Whitfield was 'a fine large man of above six feet; the teeth those of an adult about forty or fifty years of age'. Later a Dr Pridham was evidently employed to scrutinise Cunnington's skeletal material.

Cunnington usually measured intact long bones and occasionally gave skull dimensions. He was sometimes vague about the burial attitude of skeletons — though he usually indicated the orientation — but his silence on this point perhaps suggests that they were usually crouched. Sometimes he writes of bodies 'buried with the legs drawn up in the usual early manner', or with the 'leg bones doubled up'. Some of the round barrows dug by Cunnington, particularly on the Ridgeway, covered rich and important burials, some of them secondaries. Perhaps the most famous was the Clandon Barrow, which he described as 'a handsome cone, with very steep sides', forming 'a prominent object for miles around'. In various positions among a foot-thick cairn deep in this mound he found a fine series of gravegoods in apparent association with an urn, 'crushed perfectly flat upon a thin stratum of ashes and small flints'. The relics included a lozenge-shaped plate of sheet gold, an amber cup in pieces, a 'handsome jet ornament that may have been the head of a sceptre' (actually a shale macehead with gold bosses), a broken miniature cup and a broken bronze dagger with fragments of its wooden sheath. These exotic personal ornaments have strong affinities with the objects from the Bush Barrow disinterred by Hoare and William Cunnington.

Although Cunnington never reached the primary burial in the Clandon Barrow, evidence from similar-type barrows on the Ridgeway suggests that the original interment would probably have turned out to be a crouched skeleton in a kistvaen. Perhaps this point may one day be settled by a future excavation of this massive mound. Ridgeway 7 also produced interesting gravegoods. At only 18in depth was a cremation with two grooved bronze daggers, one six-riveted, the other four. There was also 'a bronze celt of the earliest type with a small piece of textile fabric still adhering to it', and 'two gold ornaments of elegant oval shapes', together with part of a twin-riveted bronze dagger. Incidentally, the two grooved daggers were six-riveted and the third was in fact three-riveted. The two gold ornaments were pommel-mountings. Eight feet below this interment was a skeleton with a three-riveted bronze dagger. Below this skeleton was a cairn 7ft high and 13ft in diameter resting on the chalk. Among the cairn stones and the surrounding earth were a series of objects including, 'a bone ornament with four small holes, cut probably for rivets, and a narrow oblong perforation in its centre' (a pommel), a faceted macehead fashioned from a pebble, a 'very fine polished flint celt', a fragment of a second axe, a flint saw, scrapers, a bone needle, a piece of decorated pottery and animal and bird bones. Finally, two feet below the old ground chalk surface was a massive stone cist, with a capstone 5ft 2in long and 4ft wide, covering a decomposed and disconnected skeleton.

Another interesting Ridgeway barrow was Cunnington's number 1. This barrow, 56ft in diameter, had been much lowered by agricultural operations. At the centre, forming a circle 10ft in diameter with an 8ft-wide entrance at the south-east, was a setting of 22 stones. Inside the circle were two kistvaens. The south-eastern one was stone-lined, and a central stone helped support the main capstone. It contained two skeletons with food vessels. The north-western cist was well built — 'the stones composing it were carefully and exactly fitting, presenting an appearance as if they had been tooled, so nicely had the natural fractures been selected'. It contained the scattered broken bones of a 15-year-old.

Cunnington met with other well-furnished graves. One at Whitfield contained a skeleton in a chalk-cut pit with a twin-riveted dagger. 'The fine bright green colour of this when first seen, before exposure to the air, was most beautiful.' He gave measurements of most graves and cists, and usually described the pottery vessels he unearthed in some detail. Sometimes the burial ceremony was discussed, as at a barrow near Hardy's Monument. He felt that a 'body was entirely consumed by the burning of heather and gorse; the whole of the ashes were then put in the bottom of the excavation, fresh fuel added, and then the stones heaped upon the still burning fire'.

On one occasion Cunnington's sharp eyes noticed a barrow being destroyed at Lewell whilst he was on a train journey! 'As I passed this barrow by rail,' he wrote, 'I happened to see that it was being taken entirely away for the flints in it.' He hastened to the spot as soon as he could, employing the labourers 'for some hours', before finding an urn. Most of Cunnington's work occupied the years 1878–88. He seems to have been a reasonably careful barrow opener as far as his notes suggest, although he was hardly distinguished by the highest standards; the main pity is that his manuscripts were never published. They, and the watercolour sketches of pottery, artifacts, barrow plans and sections, plus a good map of his Ridgeway barrows remain housed in the Dorset County Museum and it seems unlikely that they will ever appear in print.

9 Derbyshire

The torch lit by the Batemans and their associates was carried on well into the later years of the nineteenth century. One of Bateman's already mentioned personal friends, Llewellynn Jewitt (1816–86) carried on the work of digging the Peak District cairns, assisted by John Fossick Lucas (1838–72), a young, leisured, country gentleman. In later years Jewitt wrote a series of books and articles on archaeology including *Grave Mounds and Their Contents* (1870) and *Half-hours with Some English Antiquities* (1877). A paper on his earlier excavations in 1862 appeared in the *Reliquary*. Jewitt's skill as an artist is again seen to advantage in the numerous illustrations accompanying the report, including ground plans of the Hitter Hill cairn. Although the varying shape and direction of the trenches in the plans evokes a shudder, the report was precise and clearly written. Jewitt promised further accounts of future investigations, and it is clear that he and Lucas did far more, but apart from a couple of papers by the latter in later volumes of the *Reliquary*, only a few terse notes in the former's diaries serve to tell us what was done and what was hoped to be done. On Stanton Moor were some mutilated cairns of which Jewitt promised, 'I shall reopen some of them at least.' Elsewhere in his diaries he scribbles notes such as 'Hungry Bentley to open a barrow. Found a cinerary urn, a jet pendant, two jet beads and a bronze dagger,' and, 'at barrows at Tinker's Lane till noon'. He also reveals with some warmth the partial opening of a cairn on Hollington Pastures. A skeleton partly cleared and then covered up till the following day was dug up and smashed by the local gamekeeper, probably in the illusory hope of finding treasure.

In view of Jewitt's comments on the necessity for careful excavation and the full publication of the results (printed in the *Reliquary*), his failure to produce more than a few tantalising and desultory lines on his later openings (culled from selections from Jewitt's diaries in William Henry Goss's *Life and Death of Llewellynn Jewitt*, published in 1889) is a great disappointment. Lucas was no better. He died in 1872 at the early age of 34, leaving a considerable collection of prehistoric relics that passed to the British Museum. Apart from his two papers in the *Reliquary*, only inadequate notes in the British Museum Catalogue locate the origin of the finds. These casual jottings are all the harder to appreciate when one realises that Lucas and Jewitt had Bateman's example of careful description and reasonably accurate location of excavated sites to guide them. Entries such as 'found on Monyash Moor' considerably lessen the value of much of Lucas's collection, since many of his sites have been forever lost. This lack of adequate positioning and description of the majority of Lucas's sites is all the more sad, since his published papers are carefully written, full accounts of the operations, with illustrations and concise details of mound materials and of the burials and their associations. Some of the prehistoric skulls he found were reported on by Dr J. Barnard Davis.

55 *Bust of Lewellynn Jewitt (1816–86). Though a barrow digger himself, Jewitt is best remembered as an illustrator, founder of the pioneering antiquarian magazine* Reliquary, *and for his extensive publications on archaeological topics.*

A further local excavator busy in the 1860s was Benjamin Bagshawe, another country gentleman of leisure. Bagshawe dug a number of Peak cairns around Bradwell, but left only one published report of his doings plus a packet of notes describing, mostly inadequately, a series of other desultory diggings, including that of the Hazlebadge round cairn in 1866 and 1868 which contained 30 or more inhumation burials. One skull was reported on by Dr George Rolleston of Oxford, who later worked with Canon Greenwell in his extensive investigations.

One of the most entertaining amateur excavators in Derbyshire in the 1870s was Rooke Pennington (1844–87), a solicitor who had a holiday home and museum in Castleton. Born in Leeds, Pennington practised first in Manchester before settling in Bolton in 1870. He set up in partnership with a Mr Ramwell, but found himself doing the bulk of the work, which included acting as legal agents to the local Conservative Party. In 1873 Pennington suffered an attack of 'congestion of the brain' and there is little doubt that his increasing load of professional and political exertion took their toll.

Archaeology and geology were doubtless his salvation. With a small band of enthusiasts, he dug both on the limestone uplands and the gritstone moorlands. A good geologist, Pennington had an interest in caves and rock shelters, and did some work on the Palaeolithic era. He wrote a gossipy little book, *Barrows and Bone Caves of Derbyshire*, published in 1877. The book is delightfully easy to read, and includes the then latest prehistoric terminology; the periods are labelled 'Palaeolithic', 'Neolithic', 'Bronze Age', giving the work a somewhat modern ring. Pennington's writings show that he was obviously an enthusiast, keenly interested in what his friends labelled his 'body snatching' activities. He opened many cairns and from his book one builds up a picture of some rather rough and ready activity; comments include such disquieting terms as 'beginning the attack', 'breaking into cists' and 'pulling tumuli to pieces'! Sadly he fell into the trap of letting hired labourers loose on burial-mounds with no adequate safeguards. Thus on one occasion an urn was found intact in a mound, 'but was unfortunately completely broken by the men before I got to the place'.

Pennington wrote quite candidly of 'turning sulky' when a moorland cairn proved to have been previously rifled, and of 'groping home' when mists suddenly fell during one damp day's work. Once a young bull interrupted a dig near Bradwell by chasing off the workers. Pennington noted that it 'had a decided objection to archaeological research'. On another occasion 'the fair sex' enlivened a cairn opening on Gautries Hill. They came in a party from the Manchester Field Naturalists and Archaeological Society. The account reads as a rather light-hearted occasion, as 'a couple of workmen started by cutting a way towards the centre. Then a crowd of zealous volunteers took possession'. In terms of time some digs took a while to finish. One cairn called Dirt Low 'took several days to fairly turn over'!

The young solicitor noted in his writings that his barrow-digging parties were usually small in number. His particular companion, John Tym was usually present, sometimes with his brother Charles ('patient, careful old Charles'), plus occasionally 'Tom and Jake, or Jack and Mike', and a farmer friend or two or a clerical acquaintance who 'would help us out with our meat pies or bottled beer' from time to time. His 'body snatching' proclivities, as his 'scoffing friends', called them, seem relaxed and amiable affairs, and were doubtless looked forward to by all who were invited.

56 *View of the Hitter Hill cairn opened by Jewitt and J.F. Lucas in 1862. Note the haphazard holes sunk at various places in the mound.*

Although Pennington's work hardly seems distinguished by the most exacting standards, he proved an intelligent observer who had some cogent comments to make on cairns and their constructors. He noted the 'Three Age' system of prehistory, and suggested that a 'copper' age existed before the coming of true bronze. Some of his thoughts evoke a smile, and one paragraph must have crystallised the thoughts of many a nineteenth-century archaeologist when work was hard and finds few. He wrote:

> Barrow digging is something like bottom fishing. There is plenty of fun and excitement when you are fairly in for a good thing, when every moment something is turned up, and you bless the generous mourners who have left so much for you to rejoice over. But when work is hard and results small, you lie down and smoke your pipe and watch your comrades, and begin to think profanely of the memory of the Prehistoric niggards. And as bone-hunting is the uncertainest lottery that ever was, your state of mind is variable.

Later on he writes:

> Barrow digging is not all success. Sometimes you meet with a regular 'sell', as though some Neolithic humorist had prepared some elaborate practical joke for your especial benefit. You may meet at a most promising cover and draw a blank. Or you may find a miserable remnant of bone, or of pottery hardly to be recognised from the peat in which it had decayed.

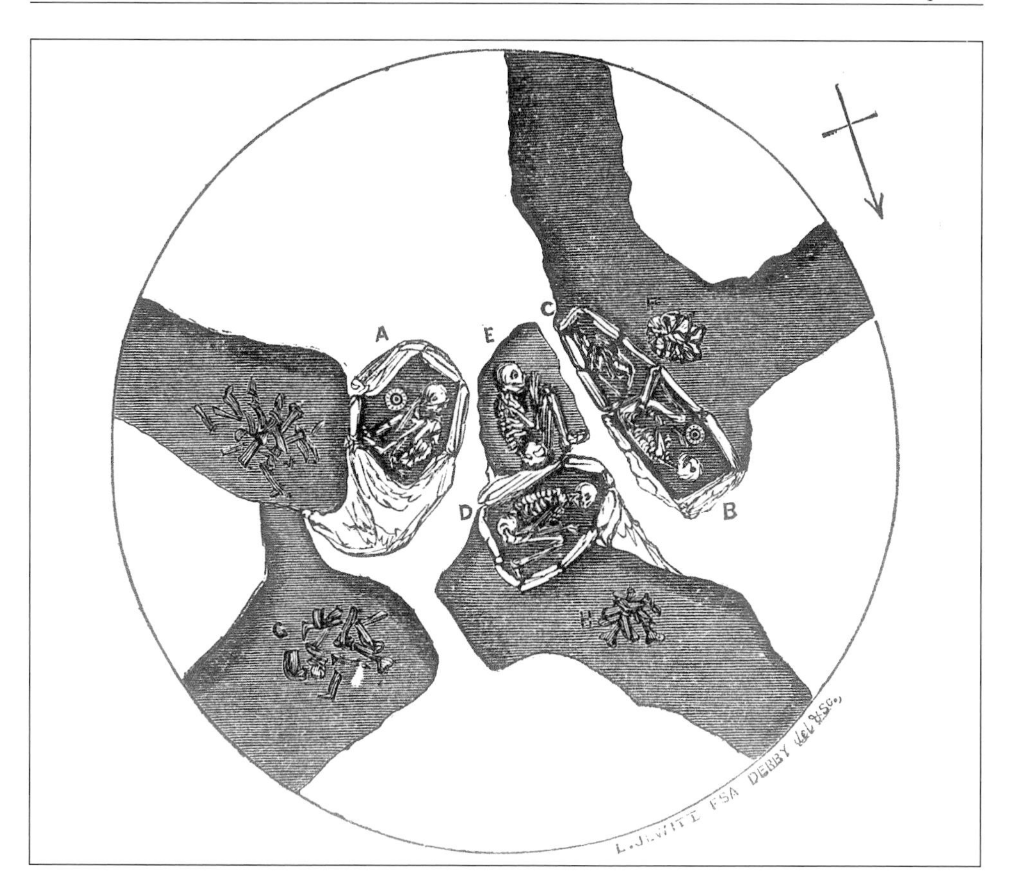

57 *Jewitt's plan of the trenches cut into Hitter Hill contrasts unfavourably with his earlier ones of Bateman's operations (Plates 32 and 36).*

One barrow in particular proved a great disappointment:

> Never did a likelier barrow present itself to the ardent archaeologist. We went to work with a will; shovel and pick, and all the barrow opening paraphernalia were put in action; every stone was carefully taken down, every shovelful of earth was religiously put through the sieve, and we found — nothing. The barrow was just like any other, built up in the same fashion, but it yielded not a sign of its purpose.

Pennington's descriptions of his barrow-digging activities flow in a brisk narrative, taking his reader through the stages involved in the work and drawing useful conclusions respecting the erection of the mounds and the status of the skeletons they covered. In another part of the book he proves a capable observer and commentator on antiquities. He inferred the greater antiquity of long barrows and cairns over round ones (Jewitt favoured an opposite view) and suggested, bravely for those days, that the Neolithic

59 *John Ward (1856–1922), a careful and painstaking barrow opener, did his early work in his native Derbyshire. Later, while curator of Cardiff Museum, he excavated burial mounds and other sites in South Wales. His successor at the museum was Mortimer Wheeler.*

population of Britain was not slaughtered and enslaved by immigrant Early Bronze Age communities (the prevailing contemporary theory). He wrote:

> I should rather incline to the conclusion that if bronze were introduced by an invading race the bronze-using conquerors did not exterminate the Neolithic race, but intermingled both their blood and their customs with the stone-using people . . . the same races, possessing the same customs . . . occupied the district both in Neolithic and Bronze times.

Pennington's book unfortunately contains not a single plan or diagram, but it is still a humorous, eminently readable account of his work. As a digger he was a typical product of his time, but his grasp of new theories and terminology, coupled with his insight into some of the problems and theories respecting barrows and the society which erected them marks him as someone worth remembering, someone a little further advanced in certain ways than many of his contemporaries. According to his obituary he had 'been in failing health for some years', especially after the disappearance of his partner in the practice. He died at the early age of 42, and his little museum, cared for by John Tym (1829–1901) who himself dug a few cairns around Castleton, was finally dispersed in 1888 and sold to Bolton Museum.

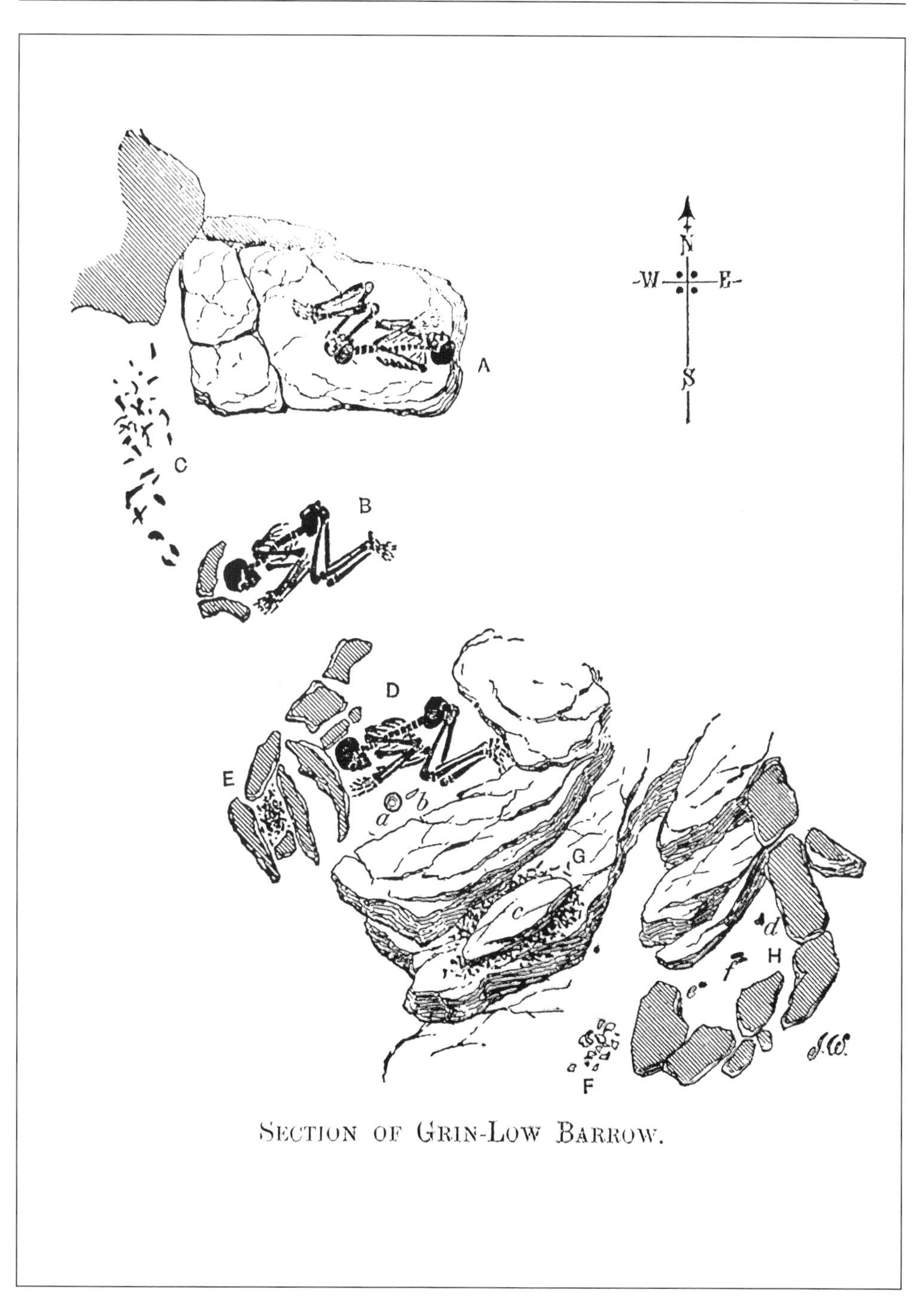

58 *Plan of the Grin Low cairn drawn by John Ward who provided the illustrations for Micah Salt's barrow digs around Buxton. Ward was one of the best in this field and his work, as seen here, shows his skills to perfection.*

In the final decade of the nineteenth century the Salts, father and son, carried out some cairn openings around Buxton. Micah Salt, the father (1847–1915), had his interest in archaeology kindled when as a boy he had seen some men exploring a barrow on Hollinsclough Moor in 1862. Impelled by curiosity, he himself continued the opening when the party had gone. Digging a foot deeper than his predecessors had penetrated, the young Salt found a cremation with a bronze brooch. Only years afterwards did he find out that the digging party he had observed was led by Jewitt and Lucas.

Micah Salt was born in Macclesfield, where he worked as a silk-weaver. He came to Buxton and eventually set up in business as a tailor and outfitter. As well as an antiquary, he was an ornithologist and a collector of old paintings, old Staffordshire china and engravings. He was a member of the Free Library Committee and spent a good deal of his time in the library and its attendant museum. He was described, rather patronisingly, as 'an intelligent tradesman' by the supercilious Reverend Charles Cox. Salt began his archaeological explorations by digging in caves and rock shelters. He was a self-taught archaeologist who learned by experience. His labour force was largely provided by 'the assistance cheerfully given by his sons', of whom he fathered four. Salt dug at some dozen cairns, most of them recorded by Turner in his work *Ancient Remains near Buxton — the archaeological explorations of Micah Salt*, published in 1899.

Turner's work showed that Salt had some system; his digging was reasonably prosecuted since much of it was guided by John Ward (1856–1922), an enlightened archaeologist, born in Derby, and who opened a few cairns in his native county, including one chambered barrow, at Harborough. He also wrote the prehistoric chapter in the *Victoria County History of Derby*. Ward, who was curator of Cardiff Museum, carried out the first scientific investigation of a chambered long barrow — the Tinkinswood mound in Glamorgan in 1914. Ward wrote up most of the accounts of Salt's digs, drew the plans, sections and gravegoods from Salt's notes and was doubtless responsible for the full, precise descriptions of the cairn structures and the burials unearthed, which were reprinted in Turner's book from their original place in the *Proceedings of the Society of Antiquaries*. Most of the mounds were trenched in various directions; some were reinvestigated from time to time; one mound on Hollinsclough had been previously opened by Bateman, who had left a lead tablet to record his dig. Most of Salt's cairns were circular ones; he only explored one chambered tomb, the Neolithic round cairn at Fivewells. The craters and depressions still visible in the mound are believed to date from his investigations in 1899.

10 Cornwall

The burial mounds of Cornwall have suffered as much as any during the past few centuries. Many were opened without any record and many were effaced by the agricultural operations of the eighteenth and nineteenth centuries. In his *Naenia Cornubiae* (1872) William Copeland Borlase writes:

> It has happened that out of the many thousand barrows strewn over the wilder portions of the Duchy, more than one half have been opened, as a mere matter of curiosity, by persons leaving no record whatever of the result. Added to all this, the recent reclamation of waste lands, particularly in the Western districts, and the ever fluctuating mineral interests, which literally turn the surface of the county inside out for miles together, have combined to obliterate those traces of the ancient inhabitants.

One of the earliest recorded digs in Cornish history was noted by Norden in his survey of Cornwall (1584). A few years before 1584, Norden recalled a man called Gyldye opening a barrow at Withiel. He wrote a good description of a cist burial containing an urn cremation, considering the time at which it was written:

> As he was digging a borowe or burial hill, whereof ther are manie in theis partes, in the time of the Romish, Saxon and Danish warrs occasioned to be made, founde in the bottome of the borow, 3 whyte stones sett triangularly as pillars supportinge another stone nere a yard square, and vnder it an earthern Pott verie thyck, haulfe full of black slymye matter, seeminge to have been the congealed ashes of some worthy man, ther comitted in this manner to his buriall; the like where of have been, and are often founde ...

The field monuments of Cornwall were among the first of any to be described in detail, by William Borlase who wrote his *Antiquities of Cornwall* in 1754. For its time it was an outstanding study, being written in all seriousness as a substitute for the opportunities of classical learning, which had eluded its writer early in life.

William Borlase himself carried out barrow investigations in the 1750s. He dug one barrow at Trelowarren in 1751, and the description of the mound construction and interments is, for its day, of a high order. Of the mound's structure he wrote:

> throughout the whole composition of the barrow, I observed . . . clay, mould, wood ashes, and rubble-stone, mixed very disorderly, so that there can be no doubt that the people who formed the Barrow took indifferently of the mould and clay that lay nearest at hand.

Of the burials he remarks:

> there were found two Urns, one on each side, with their mouths turned downwards, and small bones and ashes inclosed . . . the Urns were placed on the yellow clay . . . then the black vegetable mould was placed round about the Urns.

In 1756 he worked on some of the Scillonian entrance graves on the island of St Mary's. 'We pitched upon a hill where there are many of these Barrows,' he wrote, 'with a design to search them, and on Wednesday June the third, having hired some soldiers, proceeded to open them'. He drew ground plans of two of the mounds he dug — perhaps the first ground plans of excavated barrows known to English archaeology. Of these diggings he notes, 'In the first (barrow) we found no bones, or urns, but some strong unctuous earth, which smelt cadaverous . . . there was a passage into it . . . it was walled on each side with masonry and mortar'.

The most important work on Cornish tumuli in the nineteenth century was undertaken by William Copeland Borlase, country gentleman and Cornish MP. He described his work in *Naenia Cornubiae*, printed in 1872, a work considered at the time to be below the general standards of contemporary archaeological literature. His later work was published in *Archaeologia* 49. He mentioned in the latter paper that he had dug 'upwards of two hundred sepulchral mounds of various kinds' in Cornwall, but unfortunately he left details of only some 22. Much of his book is taken up by descriptions of the 'cromlechs', or megalithic burial chambers, of the county, together with information concerning all the published barrow openings relating to Cornwall that he could find. His own work is to be found scattered through the pages, with no attempt at any chronological sequence.

Throughout his book Borlase advances individual theories on many archaeological points. For instance he felt there was no demarcation line between the Stone, Bronze and Iron Ages, 'as regards the Cornish sepulchral relics at least'. He felt that the whole theory of these periods, 'applicable to certain localities perhaps, or useful for purpose of mild generalisation, breaks down directly it is considered as universally inclusive, or is applied at random to individual instances'. His reasons for this statement rest on accounts, some hearsay, of the discovery of celts, or stone axes (Neolithic in date) with Roman coins, and bronze implements with celts. On this evidence he could envisage no clear-cut distinction between the three ages. To him, further proof of this lack of demarcation was provided by evidence from what must have been one of his first openings. It was on a cairn on Morvah Hill that contained a kistvaen with an urn cremation and several third-century Roman coins; one coin was on top of the earth in the cist, the position of the others was not stated. Borlase inferred from this evidence that the cremation and the coins were deposited together, but his imperfect account and poor excavation method (a central shaft) coupled with the unlikely association of a Bronze Age urn with Roman coins suggests that the deposit may have been disturbed in antiquity, or later.

Borlase wrote some sound common sense in his book. For instance, he warned that 'the Antiquary, in the course of his researches, must ever be ready to be taken by surprise, and never be astonished to find a pet notion rudely dashed to the ground by a stroke of the pick-axe, or a turn of the shovel'. He also dismissed the Druid theories, still rife in his day, as 'grounded on no documentary evidence, and often teeming with the most absurd fancies'.

Borlase attempted a classification of Cornish barrows, by shape, following the example of Hoare. Types were listed under the heading of cone, bowl, bell, flat, ring and unfinished! He noted that all the Cornish barrows were of earth or stone — some were composite structures and most were surrounded by a revetment kerb of stones. Of the above, the 'cone' is only a version of the bowl, and the 'flat' barrow is of the type now called a 'saucer'. Many of Borlase's 'ring' barrows were circles of stones, these stones sometimes contiguous; perhaps some represented the kerbs of destroyed round cairns. Borlase also wrote a section on Cornish pottery, remarking on the typical 'Cornish' cinerary urn with its distinctive outline, pierced lugs and often arc-handled decoration.

Borlase's other general observations included the statement that the cromlechs, now assigned to the Neolithic era, belonged to a late period in prehistory. He believed that these 'stupendous edifices' could not have been raised by primitive peoples. 'The further the monuments can be drawn into a modern, and metallic age,' he wrote, 'the easier will it be to bring to the rescue the aid of such appliances, as would, without miracle, account for the erection of such grand and mysterious sarcophagi.' He regarded cremation too, as late in date, feeling that it was 'extremely doubtful whether cremation was practised in Britain anterior to the contact of that nation with the Roman world'. Finally he added a statement of Freeman's that he would have done well to study further — 'The sepulchral barrow can neither err or lie, we must be constantly on our guard against our own misinterpretations'. Some of Borlase's misinterpretations will be apparent in the following pages.

Borlase's own digging techniques were somewhat less than good. Something better could have been expected from an archaeologist who did much of his work in the period 1870–85. Of his recorded openings the first appears to have taken place in 1863 on the Morvah Hill cairn which produced the Roman coins in apparent association with a Bronze Age urn cremation. Of the cairns on this hill, one 'had been previously rifled by a party of surveyors who pitched their tent in the middle of the stone ring'. According to Borlase, the cairn he himself opened once had layers of flat stones placed over it, 'forming, as it seemed, a cone over the entire tumulus, similar in style and contrivance to the British beehive-huts'. A fair plan, with scale and north point, appears in his book, but the excavation itself was execrable — a workman dug a shaft 8ft down into the centre of the cairn. The capstone of the cist was revealed, but during the raising of this stone, the workman placed his foot in the earth inside the grave and crushed the enclosed urn! With such a primitive and bungling opening method, it is hardly surprising that Borlase's reported find of Roman coins in this cist is treated with some suspicion!

His next recorded investigation was at Tredinney in 1868. On 21 August of that year he 'proceeded with some miners to the spot, and caused an oblong trench to be sunk across the centre of the mound'. He supplied a plan of this tumulus. The summer of 1871 was devoted to opening a series of barrows on Denzell Downs. Borlase took up his quarters at the Red Lion Hotel in St Columb, 'one of the most comfortable houses in the West of

England'. His purpose was 'exploring some of the numerous barrows scattered over the Downs in that neighbourhood'. However the experience gained in opening some of them convinced him that 'their contents seldom repay the explorer for his trouble', as 'some eight or nine, though dug through with the utmost care, presented no results whatsoever'. A further one, the central mound of a linear group of three, 80ft in diameter and 9ft high, was next attacked. 'Some workmen were employed by the author to a dig a trench through the centre.' They found clear soil stratification, showing that the burial mound had been built up of dumped earth. The central burial was found by a method reminiscent of an earlier, cruder age. A workman's 'pick-axe cut suddenly into a cavity in the ground'. In the cavity was a cremation with a pottery cup similar in style and shape to the shale and amber cups of the Wessex Early Bronze Age.

Late in the month Borlase was again busy sinking shafts, this time into a barrow at Pradanack. In 1872 he directed his labourers to two conspicuous mounds on a cliff top at Trevalga. One barrow, 100ft across and 11ft high was first assaulted. 'Driven by the weather to the northern and sheltered side,' wrote Borlase, 'the workmen began by cutting a trench toward the middle.' 'The entire substratum', he continued, 'consisted of burnt earth, quite as red and almost as fine as brick dust; of this there were several hundred cartloads.' A section was drawn of this mound and its neighbour, which was next examined. This mound was 86ft in diameter and 13ft high. Again the technique was that of the discredited central shaft. 'The workmen proceeded to sink a shaft twelve feet in diameter from the top to the centre.' Borlase describes the stratification of the mound — stone and clay — and gives a section of the barrow. A large flat stone, 9ft by 10ft and 2ft thick, was bared, but the narrowness of the shaft prevented it from being completely cleared and raised, so the cist was entered by tunnelling beneath one end of the capstone! The cist contained a skeleton crouched on a paved floor with a fine and rather diminutive battleaxe.

Borlase's fertile but wayward imagination led him to conjecture that the two barrows were of a very remote period. 'There cannot be a shadow of doubt', he wrote, 'that they belong to an earlier date than . . . any other interment mentioned in this volume.' Then he completely confounds this assertion by describing the burials as 'perhaps the traces of an intruding people, a party perhaps of the earliest Norsemen'! The cliff-edge position of the barrows, reminding him of Beowulf's mound, strengthened this assumption.

Later the same year a further barrow, at Trevelgue Cliff, suffered a shaft excavation. In *Archaeologia* 49 Borlase describes the opening of a series of further cairns. One on Carn Kreis produced, with urn sherds and cremated bones, 'twelve peculiar beads made of glazed earthenware'. 'The colour of the glaze', he wrote, 'was bright blue, such as that of the finest turquoise. Ten of them are cylindrical and fluted, but the two others are larger and barrel shaped.' These beads were obviously segmented faience beads known from a number of barrows in southern England at the time. With them was a perforated jet or shale bead and a V-button of a 'substance undetermined'. Borlase regarded the faience beads as of 'native British origin', an interesting observation in view of certain theories regarding their manufacture.

Borlase's last recorded investigations were on the large chambered cairns of Cornwall. In 1874 he excavated the complex Carn Gluze cairn, recognised as a sepulchral mound despite being surrounded by mining debris. The mound, restored by the Ministry of Public Buildings and Works, was about 70ft across and 10ft high. Borlase 'caused a gang of miners to drive a trench from the outside of the whole mound towards the point where . . . surface stones appeared on the top'. The undertaking was a strenuous one, but 'after many days labour, the structure of an enormous tumulus was laid bare on the western side'. The outer revetment proved to consist of massive granite blocks set on edge — about 150 were needed to surround the cairn. 'Continuing the trench towards the centre,' wrote Borlase, 'the workmen broke through a congeries of loose stones and reached a second wall.' Borlase was unable to work out properly the sequence of construction of the mound, which was eventually found to comprise two originally domed concentric inner walls, inside the innermost of which were three stone cists, two with urns. The whole area was enclosed by a much larger cairn, into the south-west sector of which an entrance grave in Neolithic tradition had been inserted. W.C. Lukis drew a good plan of the site.

A barrow on the west slope of a hill at Tregaseal, opened in 1879, contained a stone chamber and a subsequent cist at its west end, built of material robbed from the chamber. The cist contained a superb Cornish-type urn, 21in high. A good plan and sections of this cairn accompany the account. Finally Borlase opened the Chapel Carn Brea cairn. The prefix commemorated the former presence of a small medieval chapel on top of the mound, removed in 1816. Borlase remarked that he had 'several years ago sunk a pit in the centre, which, however, never reached the level of the natural soil'. 'Not contented with so poor a trial,' he continued, 'in the autumn of 1879, I caused a trench 30 feet wide to be driven towards the centre from the south side.' The cairn had an exterior drystone wall, and three others incorporated in the structure. A stone-built tomb occupied the mound centre. The fine plans accompanying the paper in *Archaeologia* were all drawn by W.C. Lukis, then collecting details of Cornish megaliths for his survey, *The Rude Stone Monuments of Cornwall*, published in 1885.

In the final analysis Borlase represents in many ways a retrograde step in archaeology, both in thought and technique. Many of his ideas were fanciful, based on no solid grounds, and occasionally his dating of tombs and interments was wildly inaccurate, for instance his feeling that Cornish megaliths were late in date, his contention despite evidence to the contrary that cremation was a practice introduced by the Romans, and his placing of the Trevalga skeletons in the Viking period despite the evidence of previous British excavators who had shown battleaxe interments to be clearly of Early Bronze Age date. Borlase's digging techniques too do not inspire confidence, both in their use of the discredited shaft-opening methods and in the indiscriminate use of labourers, including gangs of miners. On his own evidence, Borlase dug into some 200 barrows, but his printed descriptions include only some 20 or so, thus maintaining the evil of 'leaving no record whatsoever of the result' (his words), for which he criticised earlier and supposedly less-enlightened Cornish antiquaries.

Noteworthy Cornish barrow openings of the earlier nineteenth century mentioned by W.C. Borlase included a series undertaken by W.H. Box on some mounds at Pelynt. Three of these were dug on 24 November 1845 — 'a party of labourers were directed to cut a trench 9ft wide, through the centre of the largest barrow, which is 80ft in diameter'. Clear stratification was observed and commented on by the writer, proving that the mound was raised by dumps of vari-coloured earth: 'On completing the trench, it was observed that each of its sides was marked by strata of different colours, extending horizontally over ten or twelve feet of its centre'. A rather more crude operation was carried out on a barrow at Veryan Beacon by the Reverend J. Adams in 1855. The mound was 28ft high. 'We began', wrote Adams, 'by cutting a trench towards the centre at an elevation of about eight feet above the ground.' After three days hard work, the side of a cairn was bared at the end of the trench, which by this time had penetrated far into the barrow and was many feet deep. Whilst the party were busy breaking into this cairn, 'a mass of earth here unfortunately fell in, completely overwhelming two of the workmen, and partially interring two amateur excavators'. Luckily the four were 'not much the worse for this accident'! The eventual cutting was 64ft long, widening from 3ft 6in at the exterior to 19ft at the centre.

The diggers found that several shafts had been sunk into the central cairn to admit subsequent cremations. The primary burial, the 'resting place of the ancient king', was a kistvaen, with a covering slab 2ft thick. It contained ashes, small stones, charcoal and brownish dust. W.C. Borlase also mentions a number of other early barrow openings, many undertaken quite by accident by labourers enclosing or clearing wasteland prior to cultivation. Illustrating this accidental finding of prehistoric remains was the experience of Matthew Williams of Maen who went out with a mason, searching for building stone. The mason 'struck his iron barr on a flatt stone 6 foot by 7, and finding it to sound hollow, advised Williams to take up that stone as very proper for his service'. The stone came up easily but to the pair's surprise revealed 'a clay potte or urne full of earth as black as soot, and round the urne very large human bones scattered irregularly'.

A barrow at Chickam was dug into in 1833, revealing 'about fifty Urns which surrounded the central and principal one', which alone, 'because it appeared to be neatly carved', was 'carried home to his house' by the excavator. 'The rest . . . were thrown away and broke, as if of no consequence.' Cornwall, like other counties, has suffered a chequered history as far as the excavation of her barrows is concerned. Although one of the first counties to have her prehistoric antiquities described in full detail, her barrow openers of the late-nineteenth century could well have adopted a less unenlightened approach to their labours.

11 Yorkshire

The barrows of Yorkshire have suffered from the hand of man perhaps more than those of any other English county. Those on the Wolds of the East Riding have been subjected for centuries to the slow but inevitable erosion of the plough, which has gradually eradicated whole groups of tumuli. Those in the non-agricultural areas have been plundered by former generations of unscientific treasure-hunters, who more often than not left no record of their labours.

Elgee has briefly discussed, in his *Early Man in North-East Yorkshire*, the early barrow diggers of that locality, or rather those of them who troubled to make some attempt to report their depredations. Of those, James Ruddock has already been mentioned in Chapter 5. There were many others active in the county in the nineteenth century. Among them was Thomas Kendal of Pickering who, between 1849 and 1853, gathered the largest collection of prehistoric remains ever made in north-east Yorkshire, yet left next to no information concerning them apart from records of where the relics were found. His collection included 135 pottery vessels, with two beakers, 77 food vessels, 27 urns and 12 miniature cups; some of the other pots were Anglian. Other artefacts included 26 axe-hammers and battleaxes and at least 26 stone and flint axes. In the main, Kendal confined his diggings to the limestone hills around Pickering, but only a few of his barrows have been identifiable from his meagre notes. Greenwell himself stated that Kendal destroyed most of the barrows in the neighbourhood of Pickering. The complete lack of any information relating to his work has resulted in this important collection (now the Mitchelson Collection in York Museum) losing much of its value.

Samuel Anderson of Whitby was another investigator who worked in the 1850s. He sold his collection, which included 28 pots, in 1854, and it now reposes in Liverpool Museum. Nothing is known of the provenance of these relics, although the Reverend J.C. Atkinson of Danby had possession of his manuscript notes. Atkinson was urged by his friend Greenwell to publish them. This he regrettably failed to do, and the documents are now lost. Anderson received £150 for his assemblage, and used the sum to set himself up in business. An associate wrote that Anderson 'has abandoned Quill-driving in a solicitor's office, and is setting up in business as a jet ornament manufacturer'. Apparently he was soon 'driving on a famous trade'. Anderson's area of research was wide, but just how wide no one can now establish.

The Reverend John Christopher Atkinson (1814–1900) was another inveterate digger. A man of great physical and mental energy, he had a multitude of interests, including natural and local history, dialects, customs, folklore and medieval studies; he even composed popular schoolboy fiction! According to Elgee he investigated some 80 to 100 barrows in Cleveland but only 33 of these were published. Atkinson assisted Greenwell in

60 *The Reverend John Christopher Atkinson (1814–1900) and wife pose in the garden at Danby Rectory. One wonders if the barrow-digging cleric was as keen at turning over his garden as he was the local tumuli!*

many barrow openings, and induced the Canon to publish *British Barrows*, of which he made a neat copy of more than half. Atkinson's reports of his work are scattered about in a variety of unlikely places, some in the *Gentleman's Magazine*, others dispersed in his many books, especially *Forty Years in a Moorland Parish*. The titles of his papers recall the earlier school of antiquaries, with his mention of 'Celtic grave-places', 'grave-hills', and 'tumulus digging'. In common with his rather casual contemporaries Atkinson was often less than definite about the actual position of his barrows. Fortunately his larger ones bore ancient names, and these mounds contained the most significant finds. His collection shows that these finds were mainly cremation burials. It included 43 urns, but his labelling was so inadequate that many of the items cannot be referred to their find spots. Luckily, however, Atkinson's descriptions of his discoveries enabled Elgee to re-identify many that had lost their provenance.

Despite certain criticisms, Atkinson's work was distinguished by a great deal of care and sympathetic interest. He noted that many of the smaller cairns, so common on the moors of Yorkshire and north Derbyshire, proved unproductive. 'I have opened many of them with my own hands', he wrote, 'and, save in one instance, I have met with no distinct trace of any interment.' Perhaps he included those mounds in his final score, and felt they deserved no further description. These cairn groups have often been styled ancient clearance heaps, but their proximity to other Early Bronze Age remains suggests that many were sepulchral mounds whose cremation deposits had suffered complete destruction through the agency of the acid soil in which they had been placed.

Atkinson mentioned the destruction of Cleveland burial cairns, rife even in his day. Many smaller ones had 'been removed in great numbers simply for the sake of the stones'. He wrote that one man had 'destroyed not less than thirty in the course of building one single enclosure wall'. As a barrow opener Atkinson was an informed, intelligent and conscientious antiquarian who derived great enjoyment from his 'days among the grave-hills'. He gives instructive information on his working parties, revealing that he seldom employed more than four labourers, as 'they were as many as I could fairly supervise and direct'. Occasionally he worked alone, employing his 'own unassisted labour'. His working group sometimes included his wife, a friend or two and 'two or three of my elder lads'. Atkinson himself wielded a pick or spade among his navvies 'when there was no near likelihood of a find'. Two of his regular workmen were trustworthy enough to be left as overseers, but the final work of uncovering and removing deposits was left to the parson himself — the 'precious and probably broken or crushed, as well as frail, earthen vessel was his exclusive province'. Interestingly enough, although his measure of success in digging among the Cleveland cairns was in the nature of things a variable one, Atkinson reveals that he rarely had a 'blank day'. This was all the more remarkable when he reports that most of the mounds he dug had been 'previously tampered with and opened'. 'Indeed' he continues, 'in every case but one they had been excavated from the apex or summit and were very often terribly mutilated and blundered.' Some had suffered the systematic attentions of 'treasure-seekers'; others had been 'broken into by the menders or makers — or marrers — of the highways' as they provided a handy source of supply of stones.

Atkinson recalled that success so often attended his labours that any lack of it tended to demoralise his helpers, who rather lost heart 'until such time as something happened to brighten them up a little'. Once his party 'carried home no less than eight sepulchral vessels of one kind or another', while 'a total of two or three urns from the same barrow was by no means unusual'. In fact one cairn, Herdhowe, yielded 16 pottery vessels, 'all added to my collection from that one single source'. One cairn dug by Atkinson and two of his sons had been opened on two previous occasions, once by 'a party of gentlemen from Whitby'. Atkinson employed his usual digging method on the barrow by cutting a trench 'on the eastern side . . . working inwards from about a yard within the south-eastern rim of the mound towards the centre'. To his great chagrin his spade struck through a group of urns. 'To say that I was vexed, annoyed, discomfited at such apparent proof of reckless rather than unconsidered working, would be to convey a wrong impression' he related, 'for I knew I had been working as carefully and watchfully as usual, and that there had not been any, the slightest, indications of proximity to a deposit.' His words clearly expressed Atkinson's mortification and show that at best he was a scrupulous excavator, obviously disgusted at his apparent lapse from his own, for the times, quite high standards of workmanship.

Atkinson worked so carefully that more than once his painstaking uncovering of certain mounds provided proof of their enlargement for subsequent burials. In many cases these secondary interments 'led on to not only to very considerable additions to the existing grave-hill, but to additions of such magnitude as entirely to re-model the grave mound dealt with'. He usually noted clearly the structural composition of the mounds he opened. 'No two of those of the larger size' he wrote, 'were built of the same material, or planned on the same principle.' One barrow contained a cist filled with the 'whitest, snowiest sand'. He later found that this sand came from at least seven miles away. Another mound was built of basaltic stones culled from at least three and a half miles away, 'across the untracked moor, with swamp and morass to cross and re-cross on the route'. Another cairn was constructed of clean, water-worn pebbles 'such as could have been derived from the bed of the beck . . . some two and a half miles distant'.

Atkinson decided that the constituent materials of all the larger cairns he dug had come from some distance away. Experience convinced him that the mounds were built with some system supervised by some skin-clad 'clerk of the works'. He saw in the 'houes' a 'significant regularity of stratification' involving materials 'derived from diverse localities', proving that they had been built up in regular layers, 'carefully strewn and neatly evened over the whole surface of the rising mound'. Always Atkinson felt the main consideration was 'the rule of symmetry' — 'the base is regularly circular, and the sides slope up with the graceful lines of the accurately shaped cone.' Many of the larger cairns were 'girt in at the base with large containing stones, laid slopingly'. Sometimes exterior kerbs were present in the form of a 'ring of encircling stones, sunk deeply in the earth'.

The cleric occasionally recollected semi-humorous anecdotes connected with his diggings. Once while working on the Herdhowe cairn with two or three labourers, he was showing his father how excavations were carried out. Certain he was near a burial deposit, he was 'creeping carefully . . . with cautious scraping and anxious probings of the soil'. One of his workmen, evidently exasperated at these methods, reached over Atkinson with his shovel, and 'made a fell scoop into the thick of the little mound I was delicately shaping'. This reprehensible stroke found the deposit, 'but at the expense of shearing off one-third of a perfectly entire and uninjured cinerary vase'. Atkinson's feelings were not recorded, but the labourer's shame and regret, and his tardy appreciation of the reason for the parson's caution, helped to make him in later days 'one of the most careful as well as most vigilant workers any barrow digger could possibly be blessed with'.

Once Atkinson had some difficulty in gaining permission to open a cairn on the land of a wealthy freeholder. When leave to dig was finally granted, it was with the stipulation

61 Bronze medallion showing Lord Londesborough (1805–60), President of the BAA and an inveterate opener of barrows on his estates in Kent and Yorkshire.

'that I should make over to him all the silver and gold I might chance to meet with in the course of my excavations'! Mortimer and other diggers also had to agree to similar conditions made by thrifty tenants. While Atkinson was working on another moorland cairn, a spectator eyed his party for some minutes and then called out, 'What is it you are after there? Are you laiting (looking for) gou'd?'

Atkinson certainly regarded the Cleveland Hills as his own preserve — witness his condemnation of Ruddock's digging on Eskdale Moor in the 1850s. On another occasion, he tried to prevent J.R. Mortimer from conducting some investigations on Easington Moor. However, despite his proprietary attitude to the antiquities of his neighbourhood, Atkinson emerges as one of the better barrow excavators of the second half of the nineteenth century, although he regrettably eschews plans and sections in his writings. He felt that barrow digging 'properly carried out' enabled 'some knowledge to be acquired'. He felt he was trying 'not unsuccessfully, to decipher a partly obliterated page of history'. He placed most of the barrows he investigated in the later part of the Bronze Age. Like other contemporaries, he could not date the time of erection of the moorland cairns with exactitude. He suggested they might have been built 'six, eight, ten centuries before the Christian era'. But, he warned, 'all that we arrive at, in the way even of inference, is of the vaguest, shadowiest, description'. His collection passed, in his lifetime, to the British Museum, though to the 'auld canon' it was a matter of 'a little regret' that the relics were 'not all grouped together as a collection belonging to one definite strictly limited Yorkshire district'.

Other barrow diggers busy in north-east Yorkshire were Jabez Allies (whose collection included 28 pots, and who dug else where in England), J. Tissiman, a farmer who sold his relics in 1855, H. Denny, one-time curator of Leeds Museum and who dug tumuli around Thirsk in the 1860s, Edward Tindall, and a certain Mr Craster, most of whose collection went to the British Museum in 1882.

Investigators were active in other parts of Yorkshire during the barrow-digging boom of 1840 to 1870. Lord Londesborough (1805–60), previously mentioned under his former name, Lord Albert Denison Conyngham, dug on Seamer Moor near Scarborough in 1848 and on the Wolds in 1851. A scion of the nobility, he enjoyed an active early life as a soldier, diplomat, and Whig MP for Canterbury. He owned 60,000 acres in Yorkshire and Kent, and was an enthusiastic antiquary. A favourite expression, 'vewy intewesting', was evidently forthcoming on appropriate occasions, usually relative to barrow openings.

Ten cairns were opened on Seamer, described in Volume IV of the *Journal of the British Archaeological Association*, including a long mound which produced an unusual votive deposit of Neolithic flint axes, adzes, arrowheads and knives. It is not certain how long his work force took to dig the cairns; many of the mounds were considerable structures. He mentions one as being 'a very large tumulus', containing a previously rifled cist of megalithic proportions, over 5ft in length and breadth and 21ft high. It had contained an 'urn' (food vessel?). Londesborough wrote: 'the man who had opened the cist had first stated that it contained a skeleton, but afterwards contradicted himself and denied it'. The structure of the mound was given as 'turf 1ft, cairn of stones 4ft, sand 1ft 8in'. It had a ring of large buried boulders 45ft inside the barrow edge. Londesborough gave laconic descriptions of the materials of the cairns dug under his direction. For instance one was built of 'large stones of the sandstone of the neighbourhood, mixed with the lime rubble of the soil around'.

A large cairn on Willerby Wold must have required the assistance of a considerable labour gang. It was 105ft in diameter and 12ft high. The opening method was described as 'making a very wide cutting through it'. The only find was a rock-grave filled with 'ashes', recalling some of Hoare's experiences on the large round barrows of Wiltshire. A number of the Seamer barrows produced food vessels, but Londesborough's vague descriptions make it uncertain whether they were primary burials or subsequent additions.

A famous mound dug by Londesborough in 1851 was situated among the Driffield barrow group at Kelleythorpe. Mortimer later gave it his number 38. The workmen dug out the central area, finding a 'large vault' sunk into the ground. The capstone was 'more than seven or eight men could remove', so 'a tripod or set of tackle poles and a windlass were borrowed . . . by means of which the lid was raised'. This large cist contained a crouched skeleton with a beaker, a stone bracer with four gold-headed rivets, a bronze dagger, two amber V-buttons, and part of a hawk's head. Londesborough found 10 further skeletons in the mound, but missed 41 intrusive Anglian burials, discovered later by workmen digging gravel. Thurnam and subsequently Mortimer investigated these interments. Londesborough wrote that 'the mound being nearly all turned over (something of an overstatement!) and to every appearance being on the outside of the deposits, all the bones were collected and placed in the vault. The lid was again lowered to its former position, and after placing the other stones round it in the manner they were found, the remainder of the day was occupied in filling in and restoring the hill to its former shape.' Accompanying this account was quite a good ground plan of the site, published in *Archaeologia* XXXIV.

62 Pen and ink sketch by William Bowman showing Londesborough's excavation at the Kellythorpe barrow. A mass of interested spectators view the lifting of a capstone with block and tackle, while an enterprising apple seller has set up his stall nearby.

Mortimer later wrote of this well-used necropolis that sadly it had 'been entirely swept away and the material of which it was composed has been spread north and south to form a pathway along which the modern steam-engine will for a time move'. Londesborough also dug into barrow C50 in the same group by means of a central cutting '4 yards by 5 yards'. This dig was interrupted by night — 'as it was getting dark, further research was deferred till next morning'. Mortimer later re-excavated this mound.

In October 1857 Londesborough was drawn to the huge mound at Willy Howe, near Wold Newton. This massive heap has affinities to nearby Duggleby Howe, dug by Mortimer in 1890, where he discovered Neolithic inhumations in the 22ft-high barrow. Mortimer was convinced that neither Londesborough nor Greenwell, who followed him in 1887, dug deep enough into Willy Howe to reach the primary interments. The 25ft chalk cone, which still bears traces of its excoriation by the two excavation parties, yielded little but a few animal bones, though Greenwell found a stone slab, 26 by 23in, and 10.5in thick, left by his lordship. On its face was an inscription, recording his dig on 13 October 1857.

Elgee records that after the sale of the Londesborough estates in 1924 many boxes of antiquities collected by Lord Londesborough were dispersed or destroyed and a pile of manuscripts and maps burned on a bonfire.

Some rather uncritical barrow diggings on the Wolds were carried out by the Yorkshire Antiquarian Club in 1849 and 1853. Mortimer mentions their activities among barrows around Aldro, Acklam, and Riggs. The club secretary reported, rather optimistically, in 1853 that 'the examination of the large series of Wold tumuli, extending from Acklam to Huggate, was rendered complete by the excavations of the club on the mounds at Aldro'. These excavations appear to have been most cursory. One can picture a terrifying scene at one barrow where a skeleton was reported to have 'presented itself to the excavators'! All the pottery vessels discovered in these imperfect openings were invariably described as 'urns', or 'British vases', of 'the usual sun-dried clay'. Few records were kept relating to the composition of the mounds attacked, apart from vague and unhelpful comments such as: 'in the interior a curious arrangement of flint and chalk rubble occurred, frequently found

63 *Lead tablet left by James Silburn (1826–52) in tumuli dug by him around Pocklington. The mementoes were copies of those used by Bateman, who was his archaeological mentor.*

in these works on the Wolds'. Poor opening techniques on some of the larger barrows resulted in failure to locate the burials. The writer of the reports felt that this lack of interments 'renders it extremely probable that they were not for the purpose of burial, but raised for the sake of observation or the performance of religious rites'.

Some of the Wold barrows were dug into by Ordnance Survey officers who camped among barrow cemeteries on Acklam Wold in the winter of 1841 to 1842, while they were mapping the area. Mortimer wrote that as a boy he 'frequently visited the small camp of surveyors, and remembers being much surprised by the sight of a skull which one of the staff had taken from a small mound'.

Mortimer also mentioned the diggings carried out by James Silburn (1826–52) of Pocklington in the early 1850s, primarily on the barrows of the Huggate, Warterwold and Blanche areas. He dug into some 20 mounds and gathered a collection of relics, but left only the most brief and uninformative notes, revealing only the barest details of his finds, such as 'urn from a barrow on Huggate Wold. Oct. 27th 1851', and 'urn found inverted in a barrow on Warter Wold. Nov.13th 1851'.

Mortimer re-excavated many of Silburn's barrows, usually finding his predecessor's work to have been of a small-scale nature, often involving the opening of a central area some 9 to 12ft square. Silburn's practice, following Hoare and Bateman, was to leave a lead tablet stamped 'Jas Silburn' in the graves he cleared. Mortimer commented more than once on the careful nature of Silburn's work. One grave had been excavated 'in a very thorough manner, not always adopted at that period'. Another had been 'carefully opened by Silburn, by making two large cuts about one foot apart, reaching from near the western to the eastern margin of the barrow'. Five other tumuli 'had been carefully opened by Silburn in a very careful and creditable manner'.

Sadly, Silburn caught a bad chill whilst digging a mound on Blanche Farm on 24 February 1852, succumbing on 17 April, fittingly enough in the ardent pursuit of his amateur interest! He was 26 years old. His doctor analysed the causes of his death as 'too much study — exercise of mind — barrow opening — taking of cold &c' thus covering his available options very thoroughly indeed! Like others of his time, Silburn's excavations, though good as far as they went, were bedevilled by a lack of accurate location and description.

12 Two indefatigable investigators

The Reverend Dr William Greenwell (1820–1918) stands with Mortimer as one of the two doyens of late-nineteenth-century archaeology. Born at Greenwell Ford, County Durham, he was a man of wide interests, vast literary output and international repute. He gained his BA at Durham University in 1839 and originally intended to read for the bar. However, ill-health prevented him from completing his studies and he returned to Durham to study theology. He graduated MA in 1843 and was ordained the following year. He served in various curacies before his ordination as a minor canon of Durham Cathedral in 1854. In 1862 he became librarian to the Dean and Chapter of Durham and took charge of the large and valuable collection of rolls and charters belonging to the cathedral. He held these offices until 1907! He also served in several secular capacities, as a JP, Chairman of Petty Sessions, Poor Law Guardian, County Alderman and as an officer in the Durham Volunteers.

Apart from his interest in archaeology and medieval manuscripts, Greenwell was a noted collector who amassed, by gift and purchase, large collections of prehistoric stone, flint and bronze implements as well as Greek coins. During his long lifetime Greenwell opened 295 burial mounds in the counties of Yorkshire, Northumberland, Cumberland, Durham, Westmorland, Wiltshire, Gloucestershire and Berkshire. At one time the great Pitt-Rivers was 'his enthusiastic pupil'. Greenwell was also present at barrow openings in various other counties. For example, Thurnam recalls his presence at diggings at West Stoke, Wiltshire, in 1863; in 1864 he assisted W.C. Lukis in West Yorkshire, and in 1877 was concerned with Jewitt in the opening of mounds on Harthill Moor, Derbyshire.

Greenwell began his annual series of barrow excavations in 1864, but earlier writings show that he had been investigating tumuli for some time previous to this. In a letter to Albert Way, dated 6 December 1847, he describes a rather bleak and bizarre occasion when he:

> opened a barrow near Chollerton. Found two bodies, one in an urn, sadly broken and decayed, with a central cist, in which were the very trifling remains of a body. Nothing had been buried with any of these bodies. The snow was six inches deep on the Ground, and a high wind, so you may imagine the work was done under difficulties. The cist was examined by candle-light, and the scene was a very picturesque one, the workmen standing round in the partial light, some fine old bushes waving above us, and myself on my knees, with a candle held in front of me, discussing the mouldering remains . . .

64 *The Reverend William Greenwell (1820–1918), minor canon of Durham Cathedral and the Grand Old Man of barrow openers. He dug some 300 between 1847 and 1901, spread over eight counties, and was also well known as a collector. (Durham Cathedral Library)*

The excavation must surely represent the classic case of barrow digging under extreme difficulties! Why he chose such inclement weather for his researches must forever remain a mystery.

Greenwell penned the results of his life's work in his *British Barrows* (1877) and in volumes LII and LX of *Archaeologia*. The former has been described, with some justification, as the dullest book ever written! His style is stark and unadorned. Although he records accurately the dimensions of the barrows he dug, and describes precisely and fully the composition of these mounds and their contents, the only illustrations accompanying this ponderous work are those of pottery, artefacts and a series of skulls described by his friend and co-worker, George Rolleston (1829–81), Linacre Professor of Anatomy and Physiology at Oxford. Described as 'richly endowed, but diffuse', Rolleston had a taste for barrow opening and was a friend of both the Canon and Pitt-Rivers. Not a single map, plan or section relieves the reams of print, and the besetting fault of his age, the failure to site barrows with exactitude, is often repeated. The whole work, with appendices, totals 750 pages — the introduction itself is 132 pages long — and its lack of illustrative material, coupled with Greenwell's weighty method of expression, has perhaps prevented full appreciation of its true worth. Certainly his vast archaeological collection, preserved a great distance away from where most of it was unearthed (the skulls are at Oxford, the other material in the British Museum), has resulted in its imperfect appreciation in archaeological circles.

Greenwell's excavating methods were according to the prevailing standards of the nineteenth century. He described carefully his usual barrow-opening procedure as follows:

> My practice has always been to drive a trench, the width of the barrow as originally constituted and before it was enlarged by being ploughed down, from south to north, through and beyond the centre. I have not always thought it necessary to remove the whole of the north and west sides as they are generally found to be destitute of secondary interments; in very many cases however, I have turned over the whole mound.

Greenwell was not always present in person at the opening of barrows dug into by his work force. Mortimer mentions one occasion, the excavation of the Butterwick round barrow. 'It would have been more satisfactory', wrote Mortimer, 'had the Canon himself been present at the opening of this rich and very interesting barrow. The opening was conducted by an amateur assistant [could this have been Pitt-Rivers?] in Canon Greenwell's absence.'

In the 1860s Greenwell came into conflict with Mortimer, who had begun his own intensive researches into East Riding barrows at about the same time as the Canon. A most informative report came to light in the 1970s, among the Mortimer papers in Hull Museum, relating to a round barrow near Helperthorpe, opened under Greenwell's supervision with the assistance of the Mortimer brothers. The report was written by Robert Mortimer, who called the tumulus 'Esh's barrow' after the then tenant of the land. The mound was Greenwell's British Barrow XLIX, a ploughed-down site, then only 1ft high. At the time it presented curious features only later fully explained. Although evidently a round barrow, Greenwell found a 'crematorium', which to him had features reminiscent of a similar feature in the Willerby Wold long barrow. The feature measured 31ft square and Greenwell noted that 'mixed chalk and flint had been laid upon the bones and then fired'. He felt that the mound could have been a small long barrow, converted at a later period into a round barrow (Early Bronze Age interments were found in the mound).

Robert Mortimer's valuable account describes the Greenwell excavation (with a useful plan) as well as a later opening by his brother and himself. Although he did not correctly interpret the features they found in their later opening, Mortimer's paper showed the site to consist of a long barrow with a later round barrow superimposed, and not as had long been thought, a round barrow with Neolithic features. The Mortimers found the facade

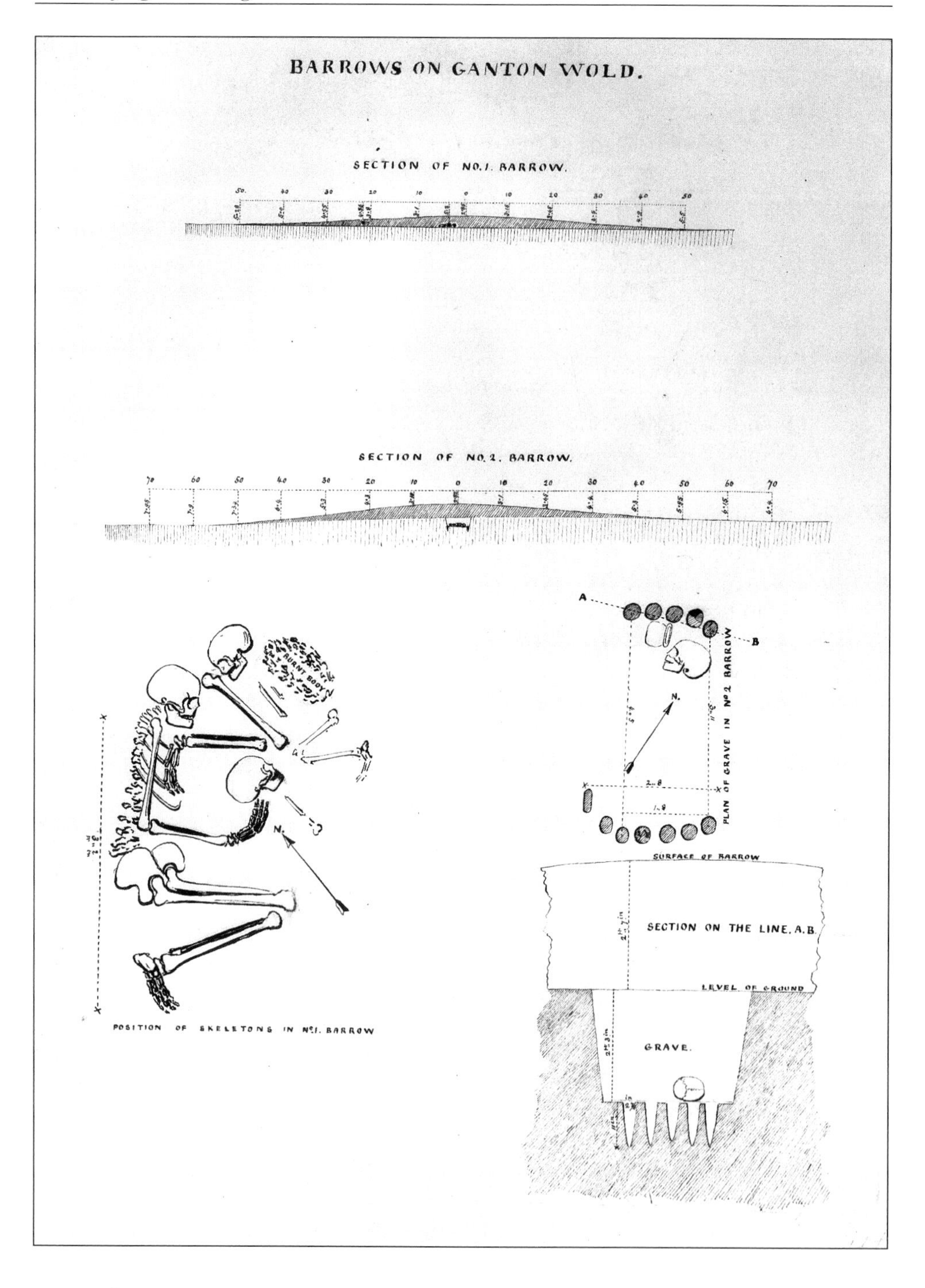

65 *Illustrations of barrows on Ganton Wold, Yorkshire, dug by Greenwell in April 1867. These fine grave plans and sections were almost certainly drawn by Pitt-Rivers during his period of pupillage. Would that the Canon had followed his student's impeccable example! (Trustees of the British Museum)*

bedding trench of the long mound, its ends cut into by the ditch of the round barrow, and two axial pits. The first pit contained burnt bones, the second, actually positioned at the centre of the bedding trench, contained an almost perfect Neolithic pot. Other Neolithic potsherds were found, having both Grimston and Heslerton ware features. Robert Mortimer also gave some helpful details concerning Greenwell's own opening of the barrow. Greenwell, and a certain Mr Evens (obviously the latter's friend John, later Sir John Evans), 'a distinguished geologist and antiquarian from London', cleared one crouched skeleton, finding a bronze knife dagger and two attached rivets. Mortimer wrote:

> Towards night, in the presence of Sir T. Sykes, Bart, Mr Greenwell and the writer again went to the skeleton to make a further research and found three more bronze rivets and a bone fastening (pommel) or loop which had been used for the short shaft of the dagger.

Mortimer felt there was a further grave still to be found 'somewhere below the base of the tumulus', but in a condemnatory tone he added:

> as night had already approached, the barrow was being rapidly completed and unsatisfactorily explored. The tumulus was trenched over with four-tined forks and shovels in a hurried manner by six or seven men as if by 'takework', a method not at all suitable for making antiquarian researches on a scientific principle — the greatest care and diligence are required with a barrow to find every accompaniment.

In an appendix to Mortimer's account his brother John wrote, 'Being one who witnessed the exploration of this mound by the Reverend William Greenwell, and not being satisfied with the day's attempts on the investigation of its contents, we undertook to reopen this mound during . . . February 1868'. As already related, they discovered the facade bedding trench and two ritual pits relating to the long barrow, and the ditch of the round barrow which Greenwell's opening had failed to reveal.

It would seem that either some words on the subject of inefficient barrow opening were exchanged between Greenwell and Mortimer, or Greenwell heard that Mortimer was criticising his methods of excavation, since barely two months after his opening of Esh's Barrow the Canon was penning a letter to John Evans complaining:

> that scoundrel Mortimer has been spreading calumnious reports, to the effect that I am destroying all the Wold barrows and missing half the interments, in fact doing the work in a thoroughly bad way. This is with a view to stopping my getting leave. His conduct . . . has been that of a rascal, and I only wish I could get authority to walk in to him. I may possibly have to get you to give me a testimonial as to my mode of barrow opening.

It does seem however that Mortimer's criticisms had some basis, since Greenwell was for some time early in his researches unaware of burials placed below the ground surface of barrows. Eventually, however, the rivalry between the pair subsided to a more good-humoured competition. Later they even collaborated in work on the Danes Graves, the Iron Age cemetery in East Yorkshire. In the preface to his *British Barrows*, Greenwell praised Mortimer's 'carefully and exhaustively conducted' barrow excavations.

Certain other correspondence between Greenwell and Evans helps to establish the former's character. Evans describes him as belonging to 'the bearded clerical order'. He was, however, 'eminently unclerical in his manners and manner of thinking, and a very sensible man'. Greenwell often wrote to Evans to report his progress and troubles. On one occasion we find him putting pressure on a lady of his acquaintance to secure a stone matrix for the manufacture of bronze axes from someone she knew. At another time he was bemoaning the fact that 'some evil disposed person has stolen my best scraper'! The pair was engaged in friendly competition in gathering their collections. Indeed Greenwell was Evans's chief rival for stone and bronze artefacts. Greenwell became Evans's most constant and vehement correspondent. 'His diggings', said Evans, 'were (by his account) generally ill-starred in weather, finds or the necessity of returning to Durham to take duty just at the critical moment.' Excavating at Grimes Graves, Norfolk, in 1870, Greenwell wrote that, 'Here I am with that accursed pit, which is doubtless the original bottomless one'. When one of the staff of the engraver Swain, who was drawing Greenwell's best bronze spearhead, broke the tip off the weapon, his next very unclerical letter to Evans began, 'Damn Swain!' Greenwell's correspondence to Evans shows the truth of the statement that the Canon was 'very downright in his opinions, and never hesitated to express them, when he thought right, with vigour and pungency'.

Greenwell and Rolleston did a considerable amount of work among long barrows, both of the chambered type (in Gloucestershire) and of the earthern type (primarily in Yorkshire and further north). In his researches into the former type the Reverend David Royce, vicar of Nether Swell, was often present. Greenwell's excavation methods on chambered long barrows appear to have consisted of exploratory cuttings, and in one case 'carrying a trench down the middle line or central axis of the tumulus from its narrower end upwards'. A long cairn at Raiset Pike still bears traces of a massive trench dug along its axial line to the base of the mound. Greenwell wrote that a chamber in one of the long barrows he excavated had been first discovered by a labourer using the mound as a convenient quarry for wall-building material. One day the man was getting out some large stones on top of the barrow when 'he all at once dropped into a cavity, and found himself to his horror amongst a mass of human bones'.

In his remarks on chambered barrows Greenwell rejected Thurnam's 'sacrifice' theory regarding the broken skulls found in certain chambers, although he accepted the 'ossuary' idea. He also felt that the broken skulls and disjointed and detached bones found in the chambers suggested some degree of cannibalism. He commented on the distinctive dolichocephalic skulls of the burials and the paucity of grave goods found with them, including a complete lack of metal. He correctly regarded long barrows as 'the earliest sepulchral mounds to be met with in England'.

66 *The photograph that proved Greenwell and Mortimer had finally reconciled their differences over digging on the Yorkshire Wolds. Thirty years after their quarrel, the pair occupy the same hole in a mound at the Danes' Graves, solemnly examining the bones of a long-dead Parisian. Indeed the former is shown handling the femur of the defunct individual. Together they opened over 60 of these small barrows in 1897–8.*

Greenwell found that the earthern long barrows of Yorkshire presented more puzzles than the chambered ones of Gloucestershire. He gave full accounts of their structural details, noting the presence of 'trenches' in many of them, filled with 'burnt chalk, charcoal and black sooty matter'. To him, these represented areas where bodies had been burned — in short they were his famous 'crematoria'. In them, he felt bodies had been placed and deliberately fired. 'Provision for keeping the fire alight', he wrote, 'was apparently made by excavating hollows along the line of the deposits.' In fact these hollows were the last traces of post-holes holding up the roofs of mortuary chambers. He thought that in one long barrow, to accelerate the burning process, 'flues had been formed . . . these rose from the level of the deposit of bones through the overlying limestones up to the surface of the ground'. These 'flues' were really the remains of the upright posts forming the walls of a mortuary structure. Greenwell was so convinced of his 'crematoria' theory that he completely failed to appreciate that the structures he was uncovering were in fact the collapsed remains of mortuary houses, often deliberately burned as a stage in some ritual — the bones of the interments themselves were often imperfectly charred, more probably by accident than as a deliberate act.

In a number of earthern long barrows, the Canon found piled material and post-holes now felt to represent some form of covering protecting and enclosing the burials. At Market Weighton there were five pits, each called a 'transverse trench', lying beneath 'a deposit of chalk rubble down the mesial line', clear evidence of a tumbled structure. At Westow, Greenwell found 'a pile of oolitic slabs, arranged in sloping fashion from the middle to the outside, forming a roof-shaped ridge'. Burials lay beneath this pile, on a 'pavement of flagstone two and a half feet wide'. Again the evidence strongly suggests the caved-in roof of a building tiled with stone slabs, though to Greenwell they were constructions connected with the burning of bodies, further assisted, he felt, by the 'cross trench' (the facade bedding trench), found at the proximal ends of the barrows. At Westow, Greenwell thought that the ridge-shaped pile of stones enabled a draught to be kept up to assist combustion.

By far the greater part of Greenwell's work was carried out among round barrows, which he opened in vast numbers. In fact his final 'score' might be higher than the official figure, as Mortimer wrote in the manuscript copy of his own work, *Forty Years' Researches*, that Greenwell 'not infrequently omitted to mention a barrow in which he found nothing'. This passage was later diplomatically deleted by the editor, Sheppard.

Like many of his fellow barrow openers, Greenwell commented on the meaningless destruction of British barrows, many suffering 'from motives of mere idle curiosity, or in the delusive hope of finding treasure'. Other barrows, he commented, had been ransacked:

> by persons indeed of better education, but who have thought that enough was gained if they found an urn to occupy a vacant place in the entrance hall, or a jet necklace or a flint arrow-point for the lady of the house to show, with other trifles, to her guests requiring amusement.

'Naturally', he concludes, 'in none of such cases has any record of these openings been preserved.'

In common with other zealous antiquaries of the nineteenth century, the Canon derived much delight from his 'labour of many years'. He expressed deep gratitude 'for the happy hours and pleasurable associations' barrow digging had given him. 'Nor can I look back', he revealed, 'to any part of my life with less of regret or greater satisfaction than that which has been passed in an endeavour to revive, in however faint a form it may be, the almost forgotten past.' All his diggings were carried out in England or Scotland, though he did travel to Brittany in 1872 where he 'had hoped to have had some howking of dolmens etc.', but his letter to Rolleston revealed that he 'was so ill with the horrible food that I was obliged to come away'. His last recorded opening was at Maiden's Grave at the age of 81.

Greenwell's 132-page introduction to *British Barrows* is replete with a mass of information concerning many aspects of barrows and their contents, fully covering in a *tour de force* distinguished by precise and orderly method such details as position, grouping and materials of barrows he dug; the types of burial found in them; the gravegoods discovered with the interments, etc. The section is a mine of information, especially with regard to the barrows of Yorkshire with which he was most intimately concerned. In fact from the Wolds tumuli he exhumed 24 beakers, 77 food vessels, numerous urns and six miniature cups. So useful was Greenwell's introduction that Mortimer gained permission to repeat a great deal of it in his own work.

Greenwell had firm ideas on the date of the many tumuli he investigated. He correctly estimated the long barrows to be of the greatest antiquity. He wrote:

> With respect to the age of the round barrows', he wrote, 'there is a greater probability, I believe, of postdating than of antedating them; and we need not fear that we are attributing too high an antiquity to them, if we say that they belong to a period which centres more or less than in 500 BC. At whatever time they were erected, one thing is certain, that they are the burial mounds of a people who occupied the Wolds antecedent to the conquest of Britain by the Romans.

Like others Greenwell's dating was at fault, and a pre-Roman era for his barrows was the only concrete fact he could establish.

Greenwell lived a long and active life characterised by work in a number of spheres of activity; by any standards his many accomplishments were worthy of several lifetimes. To his many interests in the field of antiquity and literature he added the sport of fishing and his 'Greenwell's Glory' trout and salmon flies are still used today. His dour and unadorned writing style betrays no sign of his sharp humour, On one occasion, so runs the apocryphal tale, he excavated a barrow under the gaze of a number of interested spectators. He uncovered an urn beneath which was folded a copy of the previous day's *Times*! The great collection of barrow material unearthed by Greenwell (together with that of Mortimer) appears unlikely to be ever rivalled from Yorkshire or indeed any other sites. The assemblage itself was only catalogued in 1985, when the British Museum produced the *Greenwell Collection*, the first detailed inventory of the finds from 400 barrows, fully illustrated, and with much material published for the first time. This publication allowed Greenwell's work to be understood, and its value finally assessed.

John Robert Mortimer (1825–1911) of Fimber, achieved such local fame in his own lifetime that agricultural workers of the East Riding referred to casually found flint and stone implements as 'Mortimers'. This last of the great barrow diggers was a Driffield corn-chandler by trade. In his spare time he was responsible for the excavation of 304 prehistoric barrows in a comparatively restricted area of the Wolds, plus over 60 Iron Age barrows in the once vast 'Danes Graves' cemetery, and a few flat inhumation cemeteries of Anglian date. Apparently Mortimer's desire for scientific research originated with the Great Exhibition of 1851; he began gathering collections of flints and fossils, and by 1863 had opened his investigations into the barrow groups in the southern part of the Yorkshire Wolds. By 1878 his collection had grown so vast that his house could no longer hold it. A special museum was built in Driffield to contain all his exhibits.

In most ways Mortimer stands high among nineteenth-century barrow excavators. His work was based on system, and he was the first large-scale barrow antiquarian since Hoare to prepare a detailed map showing the sites he dug. It is possible from his notes to identify

67 *John Robert Mortimer (1825–1911), Driffield corn-chandler and the last of the great barrow openers, whose collection is housed in Hull Museum. Such was his local fame that casually found flint implements on the Wolds were named after him. (Hull and East Riding Museum)*

each mound he worked on. He methodically noted barrow cemeteries, realising the importance of their group associations, and treated individual barrows as units of these groups. For its time his *Forty Years' Researches into British and Saxon Burial Mounds of East Yorkshire* was a masterpiece of archaeological method, exceeding Greenwell's great compilation, *British Barrows*. With painstaking care, Mortimer preserved all the relics culled from each barrow; they are now housed in Hull Museum, a magnificent collection illustrating the funerary practices of the prehistoric denizens of the limited area he so thoroughly investigated. As finally constituted, his acquisitions included 38 beakers, 162 food vessels, 46 urns and 12 miniature cups.

Mortimer's great life work was properly and carefully organised. All the barrow openings were, he wrote, 'conducted under my personal supervision', with a few exceptions, when his brother Robert took charge. 'With the view of preventing error', he noted, 'the facts collected during this long period were accurately recorded at the time the inspections took place.' 'I have exposed, or assisted in exposing', he continued, 'every interment in the district described in this volume. I observed everything in situ, and with my own hands removed the relics.'

When Mortimer began his extensive operations, the barrows of the Wolds had been subjected to intensive erosion by ploughing for many years. He estimated that some 25 per cent of them had been obliterated by 1843 — since that time he felt the rate of

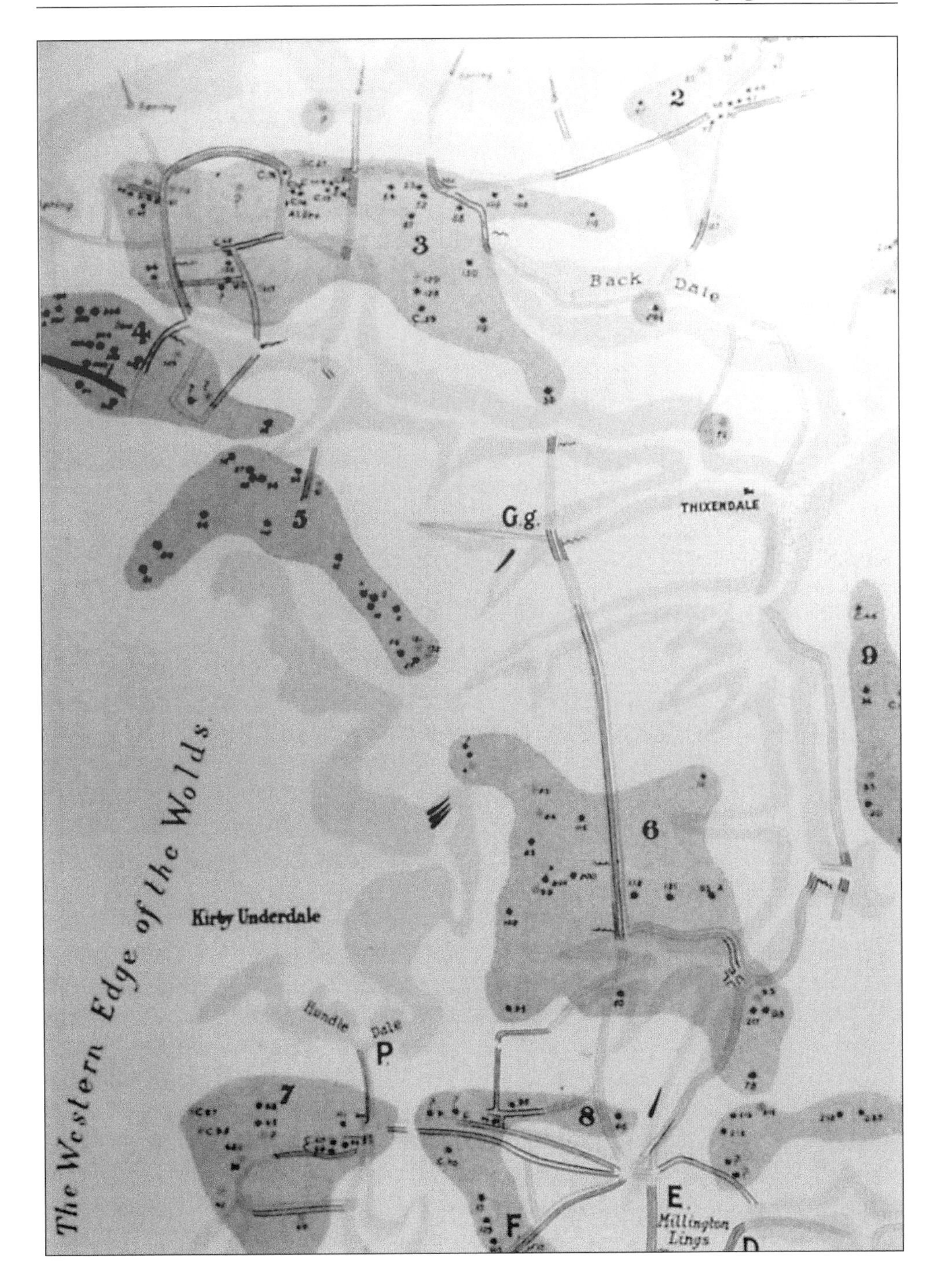

68 *Mortimer's splendid plans of the barrow groups on the Wolds from his* Forty Years' Researches. *Each barrow is numbered and each group coloured. Every mound dug by Mortimer is identifiable from this map.*

destruction had accelerated. The Garton Slack group had suffered so badly that the Ordnance Survey surveyors plotted only four barrows in their 1843 survey. Mortimer's check eventually revealed a further 32 mounds, all very much reduced and spread. His work undoubtedly rescued the valuable contents from many barrows which by now would have suffered total eradication.

Mortimer noted the group associations of most of the Wold barrows, realising that as in the south of England they formed large cemeteries. 'It is usual', he wrote, 'to find the Wold barrows associated in a group . . . though a single one is not very uncommon. As a rule they crown the heights.' Few, he realised, were concentrated in low-lying situations. Many of them straddled the lines of ancient trackways. Some, he observed, had ground plans similar to constellations of stars. Hence the barrows in Aldro group B and some on Huggate Wold were similar in their positioning to the stars forming the Great Bear. Most of Mortimer's barrows were of the bowl variety with apparently very few Wessex-type 'fancy' ones, though, of course, centuries of ploughing could well have eradicated low mounds of the saucer and disc variety had they existed in the Wolds groups. Similarly many bell barrows could have had their features eliminated by edge-ploughing.

In his work Mortimer showed a clear grasp of method considerably in advance of his time. On reopening a barrow on Calais Wold, he noticed 'holes made by stakes and posts . . . in the ground'. In each of these a small upright stake was inserted to indicate their arrangement. He continued:

> Plaster casts were taken of several of the smaller holes and it was possible to make out that some of the stakes had been roughly pointed and driven into the ground, whilst the larger — and even some of the smaller ones — had been placed in holes previously made for them, with their thick ends downwards.

To Mortimer's practical mind the two close-set concentric rings of post-holes represented the remains of a hut; the space between the walls was 'perhaps used for storing grain'. Mortimer found other post-holes in Wolds barrows; a mound in the Riggs group covered an internal mass of clay surrounded by post-holes 3 to 6in in diameter. 'It was clear', he wrote, 'that the stakes had been driven 12 to 18in into the ground under the barrow, and in three places had extended upwards nearly 4ft into the mound.' In various places on this clay 'bed' were traces of horizontal wood of the oak, ash and maple variety. Round the margin of the bed was an area of ground 18in wide, stained black, which with the stake holes represented, according to Mortimer, some sort of enclosure. He felt that the posts and horizontal wood were 'the remains of the wattled walls of a dwelling bedaubed with clay'. The stained strip of earth 'had been caused by the drippings from the circular hut, discoloured by the decaying thatch of the roof'.

In another barrow grave was a 'pointed stake-hole, 9in deep and 2in in diameter, and filled with burnt soil'. Despite one's view of Mortimer's interpretations, the above descriptions show the high standards of his excavation techniques, and his ability to describe unusual constructional and ritual features with no small degree of competence and accuracy. Finally, apart from the somewhat atypical Bleasdale circle, 60 years were to pass before another such stake or post circle was noted in a British barrow.

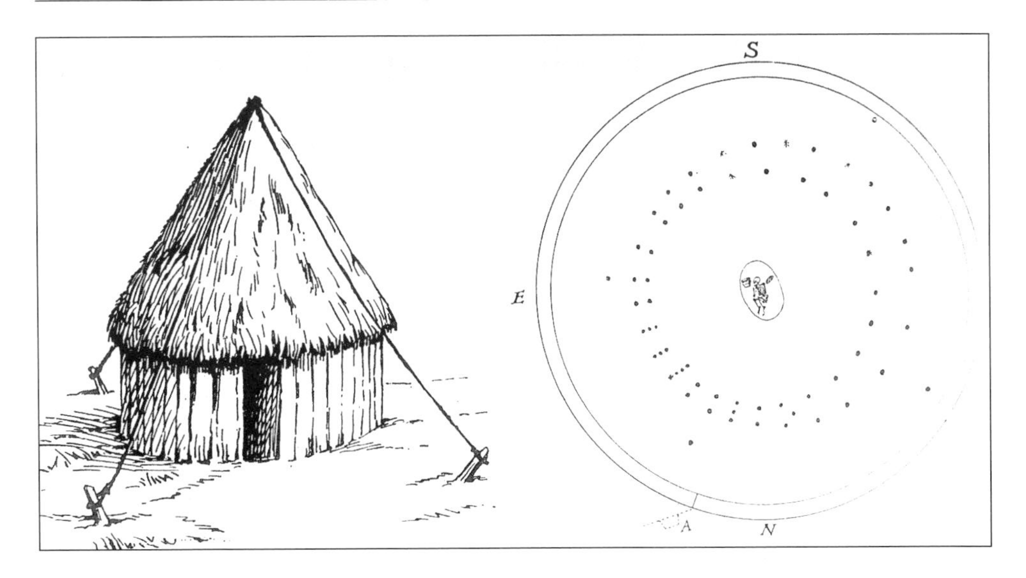

69 Plan and restoration of the stake-circle tumulus on Calais Wold, proof of Mortimer's careful work. His practical mind led him to suggest the structure was the remains of a 'British hut'.

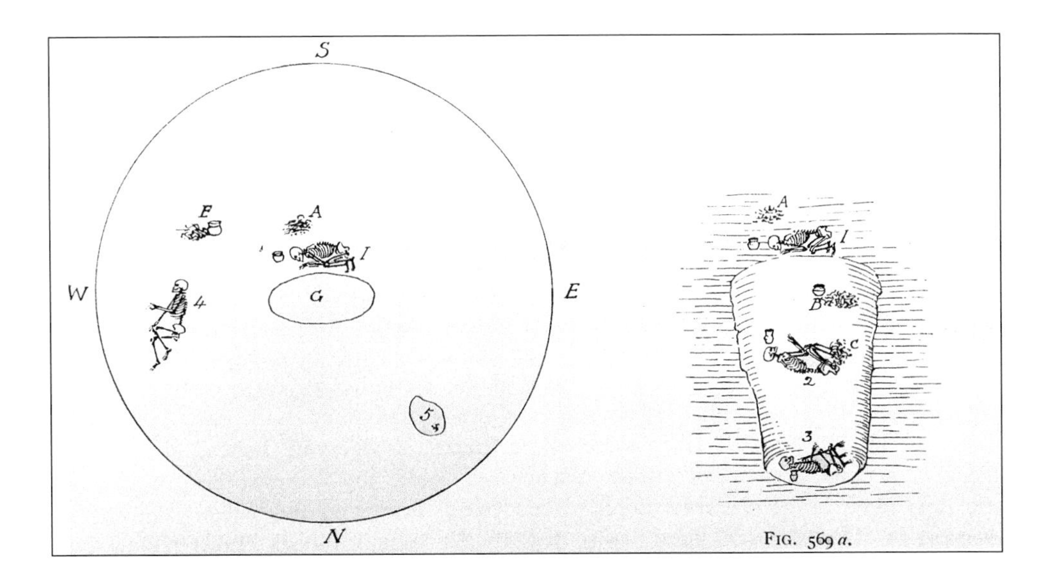

70 Plans of Barrow C69 in the Garrowby Wold group, showing the interments and other features.

Mortimer's great volume *Forty Years' Researches* was a masterly study in several ways. Apart from its valuable map, showing all the South Wolds barrows denoted by numbers, nearly every barrow was illustrated by means of a good plan, with north points added; many too were drawn in section. Most of the plans were small-scale sketches, their circumferences and surrounding ditches shown by perfect compass-inscribed circles, but they had the virtue of showing just what each mound contained. Furthermore, most of the disinterred grave relics were drawn to scale in a series of plates distributed throughout the volume. These excellent drawings were the work of Mortimer's daughter Agnes, who did the illustrations between the ages of 13 and 19. Mortimer realised gratefully that to a young girl it 'must have been a tedious and irksome task'. These fine drawings have meant that all his finds can be easily recognised and assigned to their correct find-spots.

Mortimer invariably gave the dimensions of the barrows he dug, and noted the details of construction. The Wolds barrows usually consisted of dumped chalk rubble, but he mentioned unusual details — the presence of clay for example, which had to be brought from a distance. One barrow at Towthorpe 'consisted almost entirely of Kimmeridge clay brought from the nearest locality . . . a distance of one mile'. Another showed 'traces of a tenacious earth foreign to the immediate neighbourhood'. A further grave mound revealed 'a compact boat-shaped piece of non-local clay'. Incidentally these 'boat-shaped' masses of clay were interpreted by Mortimer as resulting from the collapse of timber-roofed graves, covering inhumations interred in 'a coracle-shaped coffin of wickerwork'. He often noticed features suggesting the fall of these decayed timber coverings. For instance, a grave in a Garrowby barrow was 'filled throughout with layers of clay and soil depressed in the centre', showing that a wooden cover to the grave had gradually given way and let down the soil from the mound above.

Mortimer also reported other constructional features. One barrow section showed that 'layers of clay . . . and soil had alternately been placed over the grave in the form of a small mound three feet high'. At Hanging Grimston the mound core was 'composed entirely of blue clay . . . in places the grassed sides of the sods had been put together . . . and here and there were shewn very distinctly in the face of the excavation, by the lines of decayed grass, rushes and moss'. The chalk excavated in digging out some graves had never been replaced. More than once Mortimer noticed that 'part of the chalk . . . had been left on the old turf-line at a little distance round the edge of the graves'. At Garrowby the chalk heaps had been left piled round three excavated graves, which had then been covered by a domed core of hard, compact clay. Also recorded was the occasional presence of surrounding 'trenches' (ditches), sometimes filled with material as a result of ploughing, and often hidden under spreading mounds. Indeed some ditches appeared purely ritual in purpose and were perhaps meant to be buried beneath the tumulus as originally constructed.

Mortimer's excavation methods differed. In his early digs he favoured the opening of a central square or rectangle, often quite large — one measured 90ft by 30ft, another was 40ft square. Sometimes a trench was cut across a barrow. One, 26ft wide, was driven across a burial mound in the Riggs group. Another, taken across a barrow at Aldro, was 30ft wide. Some barrows at Wharram Percy were opened by one common method. Mortimer wrote, 'our plan in this instance, as well as in that of several other barrows in this group, was first

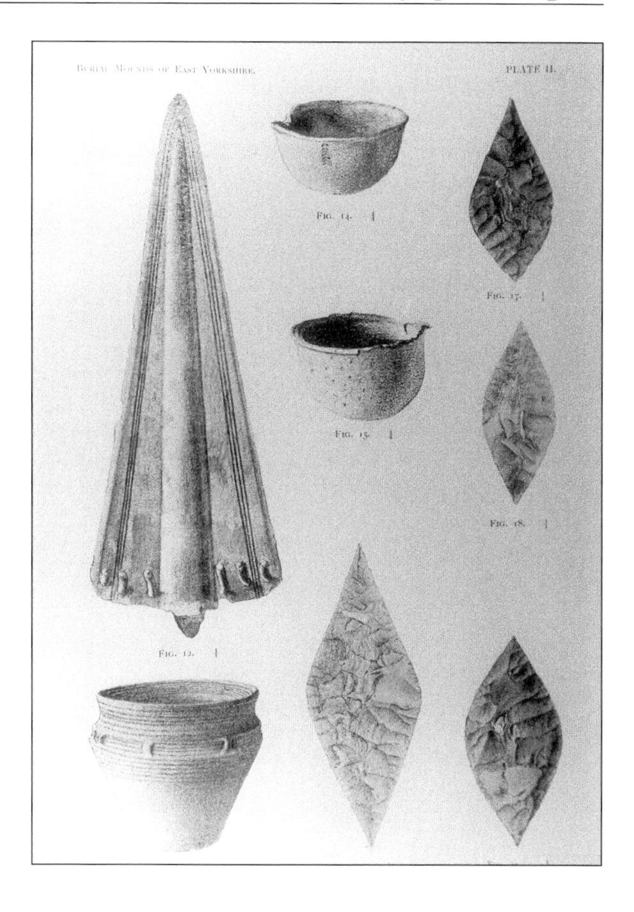

71 *One of the superbly drawn plates in Mortimer's book, the work of his young daughter Agnes.*

to cut away from the centre of the mound, an 18 foot square, and afterwards, if necessary, to make small excavations in other places'.

Another barrow was examined by 'parallel trenches, a little apart . . . driven over a considerable area'. In another, 'long trenches were cut in various directions'. The number of workmen used differed according to the size of the barrow under excavation. One Riggs barrow took the efforts of 10 labourers at a cost of £12 in wages! A barrow at Towthorpe required nine workmen who 'commenced simultaneously at opposite ends … and turned the material over towards the centre, carefully trenching the ground beneath', as they proceeded. The Towthorpe C69 barrow, 132ft across and 12ft high, took 12 labourers, who incidentally worked for 20 days to excavate the site.

Some barrows took only a day or two to open; others required a considerable length of time. During two weeks in the autumn of 1877, seven barrows in the Acklam Wold group were dug. Ten barrows on Huggate Wold were opened during 13 days in March 1892. Yet Howe Hill, Duggleby, the huge late Neolithic round barrow, took two months to open, Mortimer sinking a very large central shaft. A barrow at Aldro, 90ft across and 7ft high, had a 30ft section cut towards its centre. The ground beneath was probed 'by making trenches a foot apart down to the undisturbed rock'. The site took 14 days to dig and a further two to backfill.

FIG. 460*a*.—VIEW OF BARROW C 83, ON RIGGS FARM.

72 *Digging operations in progress on barrow C83 at Riggs, opened in 1875. The mound had been much lowered by ploughing since an earlier dig in 1849.*

After a few years experience of excavating, Mortimer began to realise that some of his early work had been imperfect, and that he had perhaps missed burials placed in chalk-cut graves below the old ground surface. He wrote, 'to this fault the writer pleads guilty during his early researches . . . and Canon Greenwell . . . was for some years unaware of the existence of graves beneath the base of the barrows he explored'. Thus on a number of occasions, and as early as 1868, he busied himself reopening certain mounds which he felt he had not properly examined in the first instance.

Mortimer's investigation methods, though extremely careful once the old ground surface had been reached, occasionally resulted in damage to interments and gravegoods, especially when a large labour force was involved. In a barrow at Hanging Grimston, 'one of the workmen struck his pick into the detached skull of a very young person on the ancient turf-line'. In a Calais Wold barrow opened in 1864 three superb lozenge-shaped Neolithic flint arrowheads were fractured by a pick, and a small piece of one of them could not be found. In 1872 Mortimer spent four fruitless days trying to locate the lost splinter! At a Riggs barrow, 'a workman unfortunately damaged the upper part of an elegantly formed food-vase . . . before it was noticed'. At Garton Slack another 'elegantly formed food-vase . . . unfortunately was broken by the workman's pick'. Damage again occurred to a pot when 'one of the workmen struck his pick into a cinerary urn, which had been inverted over burnt bones, placed on the old surface line', and in another barrow 'a very beautiful and almost unique flint knife . . . by an unfortunate blow of the pick, was fractured into five pieces'. As a general rule however, Mortimer's close supervision of the diggers usually prevented such unfortunate accidents from occurring.

During his long barrow-digging career Mortimer only excavated two long barrows. His interpretation of the features they contained was incorrect — he felt the large pits he found in them were 'pit dwellings', and interpreted the facade bedding trenches as 'passages'. The Hanging Grimston long barrow had a transverse bedding trench under the eastern end, joined to a large pit, one of an axial pair forming the basis of a mortuary

73 *The commencement of operations on the huge mound at Duggleby Howe in 1890. The cutting was some 40ft square, and went over 20ft deep. (Hull and East Riding Museum)*

house. Mortimer regarded the pit as a 'dwelling', and the connecting trench a passage to it, but the latter was clearly a timber facade trench as 'many stretches of decayed matter ran obliquely . . . and in some cases almost vertically into the pit dwelling, reaching in some cases to the bottom'. Mortimer thought the dwelling had been fired, causing its roof to collapse.

Mortimer mentioned useful aids he had sometimes thought of to expedite his work. He obtained pieces of sheet-iron to stand on when clearing out graves. 'These protected everything beneath from the trampling of the workmen, and otherwise much facilitated our work.' To screen his labourers from high winds in elevated areas, he tried 'fixing up with stakes several yards of thick cloth, expressly obtained and frequently used as a shelter when at work on these breezy high grounds'. Another amusing innovation was not apparently a great success; this was a 'specially made umbrella, sufficiently large to cover a large party at work'. Despite its protection, the diggers 'were compelled to defer' their examination. Incidentally, Mortimer sometimes mentioned work carried on under arduous weather conditions. On one day in April 1866 'the weather was very cold, with snow falling upwards of two hours'. At Aldro, 'the first few days were unusually fine, but afterwards there was a heavy fall of snow, and the weather during the remainder of the time was mostly of a very wintry character, causing our work to be conducted under adverse conditions'.

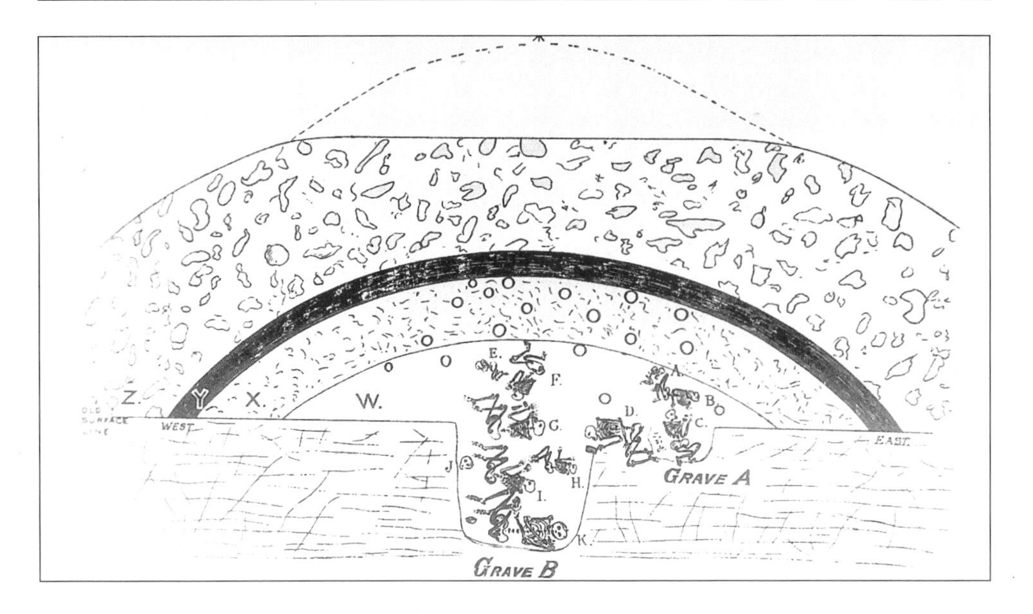

74 *A section through the massive tumulus reveals the structural details of the barrow and the positions of the collective burials. The flat top is evidence of truncation for a Medieval post mill.*

The workmen remained in the neighbourhood, but Mortimer or his brother travelled daily on horseback from Driffield to the sites. On the other hand the weather was sometimes too hot! At Painsthorpe in 1867 'the weather was so hot that at times we had to protect ourselves from the scorching sun by sheltering under our conveyance, whilst a servant mowing thistles in the same field, divested himself of all clothing, save his shirt and boots'. He also noted that Hedon Howe was dug 'during seven delightful days of the most beautiful summer England has experienced for many long years'.

Mortimer's plans show clearly the position and orientation of the many inhumation burials he uncovered. His descriptions too are full and painstaking. He commented often on the detached and broken human bones found by him in the graves in certain barrow groups. Many of these, he felt, 'are not those of bodies disturbed by the introduction of later or secondary interments, but are the remains of victims who have been sacrificed in obedience to some cruel superstition'. Elsewhere he refers to an infant as being 'barbarously severed and buried piecemeal'. His reasoning for the presence of other human bones in certain barrows, scattered and mixed with animal remains, led him to suggest the theory of cannibalism, as it was 'difficult in any other way to account satisfactorily' for their state and position. A calvarium found in a Painsthorpe barrow was of a 'peculiar dark colour'. This colour, hazarded Mortimer, could have resulted from 'a process of cooking, most probably for food'. The brain 'may have been cooked in the calvarium and placed in the grave'.

Some Aldro barrows contained heaps of human bones, apparently buried in this fashion, a mode of interment occasionally noted in the cairns of the Peak District and elsewhere. Mortimer believed this custom 'to have been peculiar to the barrows of this

75 *The careful nature of Mortimer's techniques can be appreciated in this view of the exploration of a chamber in the Hedon Howe tumulus, opened in 1893.*

neighbourhood', as he found few traces of the practice in other localities. It was proved that the bones had not suffered from subsequent disturbance as there was no break in the layers of earth forming the mounds.

Mortimer's keen sense of observation is well illustrated by an incident that occurred while he was restoring a food vessel found in fragments. 'In the fractured edge of one of the pieces', he wrote, 'were three grains of wheat, still connected in the husk, indicating that they constituted one united row broken from an ear of wheat, and not separated from the chaff by threshing.' This is perhaps the first time an investigator had noticed the presence of cereal grains impressed in pottery. Other perishable remnants of foodstuffs have since been recognised by other archaeologists accidentally incorporated in the material of other pottery vessels found in British barrows.

Mortimer does not seem to have followed the practice of Hoare and Bateman in placing metal tablets in barrows excavated by him as a record of the opening of the mounds. However, on at least one occasion he deposited a memento of one excavation in a barrow among the Aldro group. This was a metal plate with the inscription:

> April 16th, 1866. From this grave beneath a tumulus, J.R. Mortimer of Fimber, in the presence of Miss Sykes, of Sledmere, exhumed two vases and the remains of 14 human skeletons, comprising various ages.

On a number of occasions Mortimer noted the presence of spectators and sightseers at his barrow openings, mostly friends and acquaintances, and sometimes the owners of the land on which the barrows were situated. Sir Tatton Sykes and Miss Mary E. Sykes ('whose enlightened encouragement was a great stimulus') were quite frequent attenders, and the former occasionally helped Mortimer to defray the expenses of opening some of the larger tumuli, a fact for which Mortimer expressed his gratitude. On one day at Garton Slack (5 September 1873) there were no less than 17 interested onlookers including six doctors and a parson!

Mortimer described one amusing incident when the local pasture shepherd, C. Rooks, an aged, deaf individual, observed their investigations at Huggate in August 1882. After peering at them with intense curiosity, he accosted them with the words:

> What are ya deeain? Ah ya' guwament chaps? Ah ya' lewkin' fo' munney? Yoo'll fynd nowt. Ther was sum chaps dug inti't thotty year sin. [Probably he was recollecting an opening by Silburn.] They meaad a greeat hooal at wad ha' teean me up hear-a-way (to his ears). Bud they fand nowt.

In 1865 Thomas Kendal of Pickering visited Mortimer during work at Garton Slack. Mortimer recollected that Kendal had opened 'several barrows' on the Yorkshire Moors, rather an understatement when one considers the vast collection of relics amassed by that worthy.

Mortimer's book included a lengthy introduction describing all aspects of the barrows he had excavated, with the descriptions of their construction and details of the burials, pottery, artefacts and so on. For some of the suppositions relating to barrows and the society involved in raising them, Mortimer drew on many of Greenwell's remarks, which he repeated. Both felt the mounds to represent 'the places of sepulture of chiefs of tribes, clans and families, or of other people in authority claiming and being allowed a position of respect'. Like his contemporaries, Mortimer could put forward no close dating theories for the barrows among which he spent so much of his life. He inclined to the belief that 'the long barrows of this district (Yorkshire) are more recent than the greater number of the round barrows'. On the age of the round barrows themselves he could only say, 'there is much uncertainty; and I should assign a more remote age to many of them than Canon Greenwell does . . . whether or not they continued to be raised as late as the Roman Invasion, I know of no conclusive evidence.' Despite his wholesale 'ransacking', Mortimer failed to penetrate the secret of the absolute age of his tumuli.

Like other great barrow diggers of the nineteenth century, Mortimer found pleasure and relaxation in his antiquarian pursuit. 'I may state', he wrote, 'that I have often found the pursuit of archaeology, and the diversion it affords, a delightful relaxation as well as a soothing anodyne for many of the cares and troubles which so frequently beset the paths of a business life.'

Mortimer died full of years, still digging, in 1911. 'His fine tall figure', wrote his obituarist, 'will be greatly missed'.

13 The passing of an age

The beginning of the twentieth century saw the end of the age of the great barrow diggers. It did not see the end of outmoded techniques or of the depredations of the pot-hunter since bad excavation and 'treasure-hunting' continued to threaten barrows well into the twentieth century and are still not dead, despite scheduling and the threat of fines for damage to field monuments. However, the advent of Lieutenant General Pitt-Rivers (1827–1900), who in the last two decades of the nineteenth century used his impeccable techniques in the excavation of barrows on Cranborne Chase, Dorset, marked the beginning of scientific methods in British archaeology. Pitt-Rivers completely excavated sites and drew contoured ground plans and sections of them. With great care he totally removed round barrows, section by section, and after depositing an inscribed disc recording the excavation he just as carefully restored the mounds. His almost irreproachable system remained unparalleled till modern times. His thorough, minute and painstaking barrow excavations set a standard and an example still thought of as exemplary. In particular, his total examination of Wor Barrow, an earthern long barrow, can be regarded as remarkable for its time. The report included 30 pages of text, five plans and sections, five pages of photographs, 14 plates of small finds, seven double pages of relic tables and details of human and animal remains.

With the coming of Pitt-Rivers, the story of barrow digging passes out of the scope of this book. Since his time, the study and excavation of burial mounds has been pursued with increasing specialisation and skill. Reviews of modern barrow interpretation and digging can be found in the appropriate literature, falling as they do outside the range of this work.

Barrows have been an integral part of the English landscape from time immemorial. It is sad therefore to close this book with the thought that these minor field monuments so vital to the study of the prehistoric past are at present suffering such wholesale destruction, that despite their numbers they may in a few decades cease to exist. Ashbee wrote in his *Bronze Age Round Barrow in Britain* that, 'Our knowledge of living Bronze Age Society is, and only can be, based almost entirely upon the last century and a half's digging into these monuments to the dead. They are thus of primary importance in any study of the period.' Yet at present their existence as a coherent group of monuments is threatened by the ever-growing encroachments of building and cultivation, and the increasing destruction by modern farming methods. It is a melancholy fact that of the great barrow cemeteries clustering round Stonehenge, only one remains relatively undamaged by agricultural operations! Modern bulldozing and deep ploughing have completely erased sites as though they had never existed, and the scheduling of monuments seems no deterrent to the many unenlightened landowners, though recently, more realistic fines are giving the

76 *Lieutenant General Pitt-Rivers (1827–1900), father of modern archaeological methods and famous for his innovations and his careful exploration of both long and round barrows on his Cranborne estate.*

77 *Replica of the type of bronze medallion placed by Pitt-Rivers on excavated sites. The date was usually punched on the reverse.*

desecrators pause for thought. It cannot be too strongly emphasised that as an embodiment of national prehistory barrows are England's heritage and not inconveniences to be swept away, either deliberately or in ignorance.

The science of barrow excavation has travelled a long way since its inception. Barrow digging has gradually evolved from a chancy, destructive process, its perpetrators regarding tumuli as mere repositories of relics. From the earliest chance uncovering of 'yerthern pottes' by bemused agricultural workers, through the leisured activities of the great landowners with their labour gangs and their more reprehensible pot and flint seeking contemporaries, to the more careful operations of the later nineteenth century, barrow digging has developed as a highly organised and scientific skill.

There are many landmarks to note on the way, beginning with Stukeley, shrouded in his Gothick mists and Druid fancies, and his eighteenth-century successors, particularly the Anglo-Saxon antiquaries Faussett and Douglas. The real impetus to barrow opening came slightly later, from the more or less orderly work of Hoare and Cunnington, the real fathers of the science. From them the torch passed to Bateman and his associates, and to Warne, Thurnam, Greenwell and Mortimer. Many lesser lights adorn the way — the Merewethers, Atkinsons, Borlases and the like, some of a high standard for their time, others regrettably less enlightened, like Kendal of Pickering who left hardly a note concerning his large collection of prehistoric relics. All played their part in piecing together the story of British prehistory through its barrows. Perhaps they did too much too quickly — but many of the sites they excavated have since disappeared in the name of so-called progress and but for their labours the information gleaned from the opening of these tumuli would have been lost with their destruction.

The early barrow diggers form a diverse and disparate crew — landowners, aristocrats, churchmen, merchants, soldiers, doctors, schoolmasters — a fascinating cross-section of eighteenth- and nineteenth-century society. Today they hold a particularly abiding place in the hearts of those interested in the study of the prehistoric past. Digging in heavy snowfalls, examining graves by candlelight, absent while labourers hewed gashes through great mounds, poring over 'sun-dried' urns or 'brazen spearheads', they add a touch of colour to a subject felt wrongly to be dry and dead. Whatever their motives, the great barrow diggers have left the legacy of their collections and their descriptions, in quaint eighteenth-century or stilted nineteenth-century prose, of their investigations. If one regrets the casual nature of much of their work, and their sad failure to locate their sites accurately, one must remember that they were forerunners and adventurers opening up a brave new world of study. May their spirit of endeavour, though sometimes misplaced, last as long as the barrows they dug; and may time, and man, continue to spare these minor monuments that have adorned the British landscape for so long.

Appendix I

PROVISIONAL LIST OF NINETEENTH-CENTURY BARROW DIGGERS AND THE NUMBERS OF PREHISTORIC BARROWS OPENED BY THEM
(Qualification -—18 or more barrows)
*approximate date or number

Name	Published or MS	Unpublished	Period	Locality
Hoare/Cunnington	465		1803–18	Wiltshire
Mortimer	306		1863–1910	Yorkshire
Greenwell	295		1864-1901	Yorkshire
				Nthumbria
				Cumbria
				Glos
				Berks
				Wiltshire
Bateman	200		1843–60	Derbyshire
				Stafford
				Leics
Carrington	100		1845–58	Stafford
				Derbyshire
Borlase	22	200*	1860–85*	Cornwall
Ruddock	100*	300?	1840–58	Yorkshire
Thurnam	94		188–73	Yorkshire
				Wiltshire
				Gloucs
Warne	46		1839–62	Dorset
Cunnington E	53		1878–96	Dorset
Merewether	35	?	1849	Wiltshire
Atkinson	33	100*	1860–90*	Yorkshire
Austen	29		1840–71	Dorset
Lukis	26		1842–64?	Wiltshire
				Yorkshire
				Cambs
Sydenham	25		1839–43	Dorset
Mitchell	12	10	1818–50	Derbyshire
				Yorkshire
Skinner	21	?	1815–18	Somerset
Silburn		20*	1850–52	Yorkshire
Jewitt/Lucas	6	20*	1862–73	Derbyshire
Shipp/Durden	18		1840–60	Dorset
Pennington	18		1870s	Derbyshire

(This list makes no pretence to be exhaustive, and some names that should have been included may well have been left out. It simply intends to indicate the great number of barrows dug by the nineteenth-century excavators.)

Bibliography

PRINCIPAL EARLY LITERATURE ON BARROW EXCAVATIONS.

William Stukeley	*Stonehenge: A Temple restored to the British Druids* (1740)
	Abury: A Temple of the British Druids (1743)
James Douglas	*Nenia Britannica* (1793)
Bryan Faussett	*Inventorum Sepulchrale* (1856)
Richard Colt Hoare	*The Ancient History of Wiltshire*
	Vol. I (1812)
	Vol. 2 (1821)
William Miles	*The Deverel Barrow* (1826)
William Williamson	*Description of the Tumulus opened at Gristhorpe* (1834)
Rev. Charles Woolls	*The Barrow Diggers* (1839)
Rev. Stephen Isaacson	*Barrow-Digging by a Barrow-Knight* (1845)
Thomas Bateman	*Vestiges of the Antiquities of Derbyshire* (1848)
	Ten Years' Diggings in Celtic and Saxon Grave-Hills in the Counties of Derby, Stafford and York (1861)
Dean Merewether	*Diary of a Dean* (1851)
J. Barnard Davis }	*Crania Britannica* (1865)
John Thurnam }	
Charles Warne	*Celtic Tumuli of Dorset* (1866)
Llewellynn Jewitt	*Grave Mounds and their Contents* (1870)
John Thurnam	*On Ancient British Barrows* (*Archaeologia* XLII - XLIII) (1869-1871)
William Borlase	*Naenia Cornubiae* (1872)
Rooke Pennington	*Barrows and Bone-caves of Derbyshire* (1877)
William Greenwell	*British Barrows* (1877)
General Pitt-Rivers	*Excavations in Cranborne Chase* (4 Vols.) (1887-1898)
William Turner	*Ancient remains near Buxton* (1899)
John Mortimer	*Forty Years' Researches in British and Saxon Burial Mounds of East Yorkshire* (1905)

MODERN STUDIES OF BARROW DIGGERS

Robert Cunnington	*From Antiquary to Archaeologist* (William Cunnington) (1975)
Barry M. Marsden	*The Barrow Knight* (Thomas Bateman) (1988)
Stuart Piggott	*William Stukeley* (1985)
Michael Thompson	*General Pitt-Rivers* (1978)

Index